W9-BPJ-621

DESIGNING A NEW TAXONOMY OF EDUCATIONAL OBJECTIVES

EXPERTS IN ASSESSMENT™

SERIES EDITORS

THOMAS R. GUSKEY AND ROBERT J. MARZANO

Please call our toll-free number (800–818–7243)
or visit our website (www.corwinpress.com)
to order individual titles or the entire series.

DESIGNING A NEW TAXONOMY OF EDUCATIONAL OBJECTIVES

ROBERT J. MARZANO

EXPERTS IN ASSESSMENT™

SERIES EDITORS
THOMAS R. GUSKEY AND ROBERT J. MARZANO

CORWIN PRESS, INC.
A Sage Publications Company
Thousand Oaks, California

Copyright © 2001 by Corwin Press, Inc.

All rights reserved. No part of this book may be reproduced or utilized in any form or by any means, electronic or mechanical, including photocopying, recording, or by any information storage and retrieval system, without permission in writing from the publisher.

For information:

Corwin Press, Inc.
A Sage Publications Company
2455 Teller Road
Thousand Oaks, California 91320
E-mail: order@corwinpress.com

Sage Publications Ltd.
6 Bonhill Street
London EC2A 4PU
United Kingdom

Sage Publications India Pvt. Ltd.
M-32 Market
Greater Kailash I
New Delhi 110 048 India

Printed in the United States of America

Library of Congress Cataloging-in-Publication Data

Marzano, Robert J.
    Designing a new taxonomy of educational objectives / by Robert J. Marzano.
        p. cm.—(Experts in assessment kit)
Includes bibliographical references (p.   ) and index.
    ISBN 0-8039-6835-3 (cloth : alk. paper)—ISBN 0-8039-6836-1 (pbk.: alk. paper)
    1. Education—Aims and objectives. I. Title. II. Series.
    LB17 .M39 2000
    370.11—dc21
00-008293

This book is printed on acid-free paper.

05   06   10   9   8   7   6   5

Production Editor: Astrid Virding
Editorial Assistant: Catherine Kantor
Typesetter: Rebecca Evans
Cover Designer: Tracy E. Miller

Contents

Series Editors' Introduction

Standards, assessment, accountability, and grading—these are the issues that dominated discussions of education in the 1990s. Today, they are at the center of every modern education reform effort. As educators turn to the task of implementing these reforms, they face a complex array of questions and concerns that little in their background or previous experience has prepared them to address. This series is designed to help in that challenging task.

In selecting the authors, we went to individuals recognized as true experts in the field. The ideas of these scholar-practitioners have already helped shape current discussions of standards, assessment, accountability, and grading. But equally important, their work reflects a deep understanding of the complexities involved in implementation. As they developed their books for this series, we asked them to extend their thinking, to push the edge, and to present new perspectives on what should be done and how to do it. That is precisely what they did. The books they crafted provide not only cutting-edge perspectives but also practical guidelines for successful implementation.

We have several goals for this series. First, that it be used by teachers, school leaders, policy makers, government officials, and all those concerned with these crucial aspects of education reform. Second, that it helps broaden understanding of the complex issues involved in standards, assessment, accountability, and grading. Third, that it leads to more thoughtful policies and programs. Fourth, and most important, that it helps accomplish the basic goal for which all reform initiatives are intended—namely, to enable all students to learn excellently and to gain the many positive benefits of that success.

— *Thomas R. Guskey*
Robert J. Marzano
Series Editors

Preface

The *Taxonomy of Educational Objectives* (Bloom et al., 1956) was published almost a half century ago. Since that time, no successful attempt has been mounted to update or replace the taxonomy. Yet, in that same half century, understanding of how the mind works, the nature of knowledge, and the interaction of the two have advanced dramatically. This volume, *Designing a New Taxonomy of Educational Objectives,* is an attempt to articulate a taxonomy of educational objectives that uses the best available research and theory accumulated since the publication of Bloom's Taxonomy. As the title of the book indicates, this work should be considered a first step in the construction of a new model; yet, I assert, the New Taxonomy as presented in this volume is grounded enough in solid research, theory, and practice that educators can use it in its present form for a variety of purposes.

The New Taxonomy, like Bloom's Taxonomy, articulates six levels of mental processing:

Level 6: Self-system thinking

Level 5: Metacognition

Level 4: Knowledge utilization

Level 3: Analysis

Level 2: Comprehension

Level 1: Retrieval

Although somewhat similar to Bloom's Taxonomy on the surface, there are some profound differences. For example, the six levels of Bloom's Taxonomy do not address self-system thinking and metacognition as described in the New Taxonomy. Thus, one can argue that Bloom's Taxonomy is included in the first four levels of the New Taxonomy. Another major distinction between this work and Bloom's Taxonomy is that the New Taxonomy describes three domains of knowledge—the domain of information, the domain of mental procedures, and the domain of psychomotor procedures—which cut across all six levels of mental processing. This is in sharp contrast to Bloom's Taxonomy, which restricted its discussion of the various types of knowledge to the first level only—aptly named the "knowledge" level.

Chapter 1 of this volume presents a general discussion of the work of Bloom and his colleagues, noting their incredible contribution to educational theory and practice, but highlighting problems with their taxonomy as disclosed by empirical investigations and theory. Chapter 2 presents a general model of human decision making and information processing, which is the foundation of the New Taxonomy. That model introduces the reader to three systems of thought—the self-system, the metacognitive system, and the cognitive system—which form the basis for the six levels of the New Taxonomy. Chapter 3 describes the three knowledge domains and the different structures within each domain. Chapter 4 provides the theoretical and research background for the three systems of thought. It also describes the rationale for and defense of the hierarchical structure of the New Taxonomy. Finally, it breaks down the cognitive system into four hierarchical components—knowledge utilization, analysis, comprehension, and retrieval— which form the bottom four levels of the New Taxonomy. Chapter 5 presents examples of learning objectives across all six levels of the New Taxonomy for each of the three knowledge domains. Finally, Chapter 6 discusses the various ways in which the New Taxonomy might be used by educators.

The New Taxonomy is intended to be used by classroom teachers, curriculum specialists, administrators, measurements experts, and evaluation specialists in a variety of ways, many of which are addressed in this volume. Ideally, the New Taxonomy will provide a new perspective for our discussions of the nature of knowledge and the nature of learning.

— Robert J. Marzano

About the Author

Robert J. Marzano is a Senior Fellow at the Mid-Continent Regional Laboratory (McREL) in Aurora, Colorado. There he is responsible for translating research and theory into classroom practice. He headed a team of authors who developed *Dimensions of Learning* published by the Association for Supervision and Curriculum Development. He is also the senior author of *Tactics for Thinking* and *Literacy Plus: An Integrated Approach to Teaching Reading, Writing, Vocabulary and Reasoning.* His most recent efforts address standards as described in the two books, *Essential Knowledge: The Debate Over What American Students Should Know* (Marzano, Kendall, & Gaddy, 1999) and *A Comprehensive Guide to Designing Standards-Based Districts, Schools and Classroom* (Marzano & Kendall, 1996a). He is currently finishing a book titled *Transforming Classroom Grading and Assessment.*

Dr. Marzano received his BA in English from Iona College in New York, an MEd in reading/language arts from Seattle University, Seattle, WA, and a PhD in curriculum and instruction from the University of Washington, Seattle. Prior to his work at McREL, he was a tenured associate professor at the University of Colorado, and a high school English teacher and department chair.

An internationally known trainer and speaker, Dr. Marzano has written 15 books and more than 100 articles and chapters in books on such topics as reading and writing instruction, thinking skills, school effectiveness, restructuring, assessment, cognition, and standards implementation.

CHAPTER 1

Bloom's Taxonomy

I n 1956, a small, somewhat technical volume was published under the title, *Taxonomy of Educational Objectives, The Classification of Educational Goals, Handbook I: Cognitive Domain.* In the 40-plus years since its publication, "Bloom's Taxonomy," as it is frequently referred to in deference to Benjamin Bloom, the work's editor, has been used by educators in virtually every subject area at virtually every grade level. The expressed purpose of the taxonomy was to develop a codification system whereby educators could design learning objectives that have a hierarchic organization.

> You are reading about an attempt to build a taxonomy of educational objectives. It is intended to provide for classification of the goals of our educational system. It is expected to be of general help to all teachers, administrators, professional specialists, and research workers who deal with curricular and evaluation problems. (Bloom et al., 1956, p.1)

That Bloom's Taxonomy is still used after more than 40 years is a testament to its contribution to education and psychology. Indeed, the 93rd yearbook of the National Society for the Study of Education (NSSE), titled *Bloom's Taxonomy: A Forty-Year Retrospective*, documents the impact of the work:

> Arguably, one of the most influential educational monographs of the past half century is the *Taxonomy of Educational Objectives, The Classification of Educational Goals, Handbook I: Cognitive Domain.* Nearly forty years after its publication in 1956 the volume remains a standard reference for discussions of testing and evaluation, curriculum development, and teaching and teacher education. A search of the most recent *Social Science Citation Index* (1992) revealed more than 150 citations to the *Handbook*. At a recent meeting of approximately 200 administrators and teachers, the senior editor of this volume asked for a show of hands in response to the question, "How many of you have heard of Bloom's Taxonomy?" Virtually every hand

in the audience was raised. Few education publications have enjoyed such overwhelming recognition for so long. (Anderson & Sosniak, 1994, p. vii)

Those interested in a thorough discussion of the many uses and analyses of Bloom's Taxonomy should consult the 1994 NSSE yearbook. However, a brief synopsis is useful here.

A Brief History of the Use of Bloom's Taxonomy

A scrutiny of the past 40-plus years in education indicates that Bloom's Taxonomy has had a significant, albeit uneven, influence on educational theory and practice. According to Peter Airasian (1994), the taxonomy fitted nicely into the instructional objectives movement that attained national prominence after the publication of Robert Mager's *Preparing Instructional Objectives* (1962). Mager's book was explicitly designed to help those intending to develop a methodology of programmed instruction and was based on the premise that cognitive tasks could be ordered hierarchically. Airasian notes that "one might think, given this affinity, that the taxonomy would have been an influential tool in the development of programmed instructional sequences. In one sense it was" (p. 87). As Edgar Dale (1967) explains, Bloom's Taxonomy became the structure around which many initial efforts at programmed instruction were organized. However, Airasian (1994) argues that Bloom's Taxonomy was ultimately replaced by Gagne's (1977) framework as the conceptual organizer for programmed instruction. Although Gagne's framework was less hierarchical than Bloom's Taxonomy, it was more easily translated into instructional practice.

Whereas Bloom's Taxonomy had a minimal influence on curriculum, it had a strong effect on evaluation. By 1970, Ralph Tyler's model of evaluation design was fairly well established. Specifically, Tyler presented an objectives-based view of evaluation in which a program or an instructional intervention was evaluated on the extent to which it had accomplished its explicit goals (for a discussion of Tyler's model, see Madaus & Stufflebeam, 1989). The more precisely goals were stated, the more precisely a program could be evaluated. Bloom's Taxonomy proved to be a powerful tool for objectives-based evaluation in that it allowed for a level of detail in stating goals that had not previously been readily attained.

Bloom's Taxonomy also proved to be a valuable tool for those who ascribed to the model of evaluation known as the "planning, programming, budgeting system" (PPBS). PPBS, initially used in the Pentagon, followed Tyler's tenets of objectives-based evaluation in that it was predicated on first identifying the intended outcomes of a program, then measuring the extent to which these outcomes had been achieved at the program's conclusion. PPBS became popular in education when it was adopted as the primary tool for evaluating the effectiveness of the 1965 Elementary and Secondary Education Act (ESEA), which was a direct consequence of President Lyndon Johnson's War on Poverty. Under ESEA, Title I funds were allocated to provide additional educational services to lower-achieving students in schools having large proportions of children from low income backgrounds. Airasian (1994) explains that "for the first time in history substantial amounts of federal aid, more than a billion dollars a year at its inception, were funneled into local school districts to meet the educational needs of disadvantaged children" (p. 89). Given the scale of the financial aid available to schools under Title I, some politicians demanded reporting requirements that would ensure the monies were being used appropriately. Eventually, PPBS became the preferred Title I assessment vehicle and Bloom's Taxonomy the preferred system for articulating program objectives.

The 1970s also marked the beginning of statewide testing. Indeed, in 1960 only one state had a mandated statewide test; by 1985, 32 states had mandated tests. Virtually every state test was designed to provide information about student achievement on specific topics within specific subject areas, and virtually every state test made use of Bloom's Taxonomy, at least to some extent, to define various levels of skill. By the mid-1970s, state tests began to take a minimum-competency approach. As Airasian (1987) explains, minimum-competency tests were different from the more general forms of tests in at least three ways: (1) they were mandated for all schools and virtually all students within a state in which their predecessors could be administered to representative samples of students, (2) the mandate took away much, if not all, of individual districts' discretion in terms of test selection, administration, scoring, and interpretation, and (3) the tests had built-in sanctions if specific levels of performance were not met. Again, Bloom's Taxonomy was widely used as the model for designing items that measure low-level or basic skills versus "higher level" skills.

The 1980s saw the beginning of an emphasis on teaching higher levels of thinking. It was this movement, along with research on the validity of Bloom's Taxonomy (reviewed in a subsequent section), that raised awareness as to the need to revise it. A barrage of books, articles, and reports appeared, supporting the need for instruction in thinking and reasoning skills. For example, such prominent organizations as the Education Commission of the States (1982) and the College Board (1983) highlighted the need to teach thinking. High-impact reports, such as *A Nation at Risk* (National Commission on Excellence in Education, 1983), pointed to deficiencies in higher-level thinking as a major weakness in American education. Widely read journals, such as *Educational Leadership* and *Review of Educational Research,* devoted entire volumes to the topic. Many of these publications cited evidence of students' inability to answer higher-level questions and apply their knowledge.

In May 1984, the Association for Supervision and Curriculum Development (ASCD) called a meeting at the Wingspread Conference Center in Racine, Wisconsin, to consider possible solutions to the problem of students' poor performance on tasks that demand higher-level thinking. One of the suggestions from the conference was that Bloom's Taxonomy should be updated to include current research and theory on the nature of knowledge and the nature of cognition (for a discussion of that conference, see Marzano et al., 1988). As a direct result of that conference, the Association Collaborative for Teaching Thinking was formed. Twenty-eight organizations were official participants in the collaborative, including

American Association of School Administrators

American Association of School Librarians

American Federation of Teachers

American Educational Research Association

Association for Supervision and Curriculum Development

Council of Chief State School Officers

Home Economics Education Association

International Reading Association

Music Educators National Conference

National Art Education Association

National Alliance of Black School Educators

National Association of Elementary School Principals

National Association of Secondary School Principals

National Council for the Social Studies

National Council of Teachers of English

National Council of Teachers of Mathematics

National Education Association

National Middle School Association

National Science Teachers Association

National School Boards Association

Unfortunately, the collaborative never produced a revision of Bloom's Taxonomy. To date, there is still a recognition that an update or total revision is in order.

Bloom's Taxonomy—A Summary

Given that this work is designed to update Bloom's Taxonomy, it is useful to briefly review it. In its most general form, Bloom's Taxonomy outlines six levels of cognitive processes:

1.00 Knowledge

2.00 Comprehension

3.00 Application

4.00 Analysis

5.00 Synthesis

6.00 Evaluation

Each level is designed to possess defining characteristics.

1.00 Knowledge

The *knowledge* level is operationally defined as information retrieval: "Knowledge as defined here includes those behaviors and test situations which emphasize the remembering, either by recognition or recall, of ideas, materials or phenomena" (Bloom et al., 1956, p. 62). A close examination of this first category shows that Bloom articulates specific types of knowledge, which include the following categories and subcategories:

1.10 Specifics

    1.11 Terminology

    1.12 Facts

1.20 Ways and means of dealing with specifics

    1.21 Conventions

    1.22 Trends and sequences

    1.23 Classification and categories

    1.24 Criteria

    1.25 Methodology

1.30 Universals and abstractions

    1.31 Principles and generalizations

    1.32 Theories and structures

Bloom's category of knowledge, then, mixes the cognitive process of retrieval with the various types of knowledge that are retrieved.

2.00 Comprehension

Comprehension represents the largest class of intellectual skills and abilities. The central feature of the act of comprehension is taking in new information via some form of communication (". . . when students are confronted with a communication, they are expected to know what is being communicated and to be able to make some use of the materials or ideas contained in it" [p. 89]). The taxonomy does not limit communication to the presentation of information in linguistic (verbal or written) form. Rather, information can be presented symbolically or experientially. Thus, a student attempting to understand the ideas underlying a demonstration would be involved in the act of comprehension.

Three forms of comprehension are described in the taxonomy: translation, interpretation, and extrapolation. *Translation* involves encoding incoming information into some form other than that in which it was received. For example, Richard would be engaged in translation if he summarized in his own words, the information contained in a film on the formation of a tornado. When translation involves the identification of the literal structure underlying the incoming information, *interpretation* "may require a reordering of ideas into a new configuration in the mind" (p. 90). Finally, *extrapolation* goes beyond the literal level of comprehension. It involves inferences and predictions based on literal information in the communication and principles and generalizations already possessed by the learner (p. 90).

3.00 Application

The third category of cognitive skills, *application,* is probably the least well-defined in Bloom's Taxonomy. It is described in relationship to a specific type of knowledge—abstractions—and is defined primarily in terms of how it compares with other levels of the taxonomy. To illustrate, Bloom notes that the comprehension of an abstraction requires students to know the abstraction well enough that they can

> correctly demonstrate its use when specifically asked to do so. "Application," however, requires a step beyond this. Given a problem new to the student, he will apply the appropriate abstraction without having to be prompted as to which abstraction is correct or without having to be shown how to use it in that situation. (p. 120)

Bloom further explains that an abstraction understood at the level of comprehension can be used only when the conditions for its use are specified. However, the application of an abstraction is demonstrated when one correctly uses the abstraction in a situation in which no mode of solution is specified.

4.00 Analysis

Just as application is defined in terms of a subordinate category of Bloom's Taxonomy, *analysis* is defined in terms of application and comprehension. Bloom notes that,

> In *comprehension*, the emphasis is on the grasp of the meaning and intent of the material. In *application* it is on remembering and bringing to bear upon given material the appropriate generalizations or principles. *Analysis* emphasizes the detection of relationships of the parts and of the way they are organized. (p. 144)

Analysis is divided into three subcategories: the identification or classification of (1) elements, (2) relationships among elements, and (3) organizational principles that govern elements (p. 145).

Admittedly, this category overlaps with the categories of comprehension and evaluation: "No entirely clear lines can be drawn between analysis and comprehension at one end or between analysis and evaluation at the other" (p. 144).

5.00 Synthesis

Synthesis primarily involves the generation of new knowledge structures.

> Synthesis is defined here as putting together elements and parts as to form a whole. This is a process of working with elements, parts, etc., and combining them in such a way as to constitute a pattern or structure not clearly there before. Generally, this would involve a recombination of parts of previous experiences with new material, reconstructed into a new and more or less well-integrated whole. (p. 162)

Bloom explains that this category of cognition most clearly calls for creative behavior on the part of the student because it involves newly constructed and oftentimes unique products. Three specific categories of products are defined: (1) unique communications, (2) a plan or set of operations, and (3) a set of abstract relationships.

Again, Bloom acknowledges many similarities between this category and the previous categories: "Comprehension, application, and analysis also involve the putting together of elements and the construction of meanings, but these tend to be more partial and less compatible than synthesis in the magnitude of the task" (p. 162).

6.00 Evaluation

Evaluation involves making judgments about the value of knowledge. According to Bloom, it involves

> the use of criteria as well as standards for appraising the extent to which particulars are accurate, effective, economical, or satisfying. The judgments may be either quantitative or qualitative and the criteria may be either those determined by the student or those which are given to him. (p. 185)

Two forms of criteria or evidence are noted within this category: internal and external. By definition, *evaluation* is a form of decision making, done at a very conscious and thoughtful level as opposed to decisions that are made quickly without much conscious thought. Bloom refers to the latter as "opinions," as opposed to "judgments," which, by definition, involve evaluation.

Problems With Bloom's Taxonomy

As influential as Bloom's Taxonomy has been on educational practice, it has experienced some severe criticisms (for a review, see Kreitzer & Madaus, 1994). One of the most common criticisms was that the taxonomy oversimplified the nature of thought and its relationship to learning (Furst, 1994). The taxonomy certainly expanded the conception of learning from a simple, unidimensional, behaviorist model to one that was multidimensional and more constructivist in nature. However, it assumed a rather simple construct of difficulty as the characteristic separating one level from another: Superordinate levels involved more difficult cognitive processes than did subordinate levels. The research conducted on Bloom's Taxonomy simply did not support this structure. For example, educators who were trained in the structure of Bloom's Taxonomy consistently were not able to recognize questions at higher levels as more difficult than questions at lower levels of the taxonomy (see Fairbrother, 1975; Poole, 1972; Stanley & Bolton, 1957).

The problems with Bloom's Taxonomy were indirectly acknowledged by its authors. This is evidenced in their discussion of analysis: ". . . it is probably more defensible educationally to consider analysis as an aid to fuller comprehension (a lower class level) or as a prelude to an evaluation of the material" (p. 144). The authors also acknowledged problems with the taxonomy's structure in their discussion of evaluation:

Although evaluation is placed last in the cognitive domain because it is regarded as requiring to some extent all the other categories of behavior, it is not necessarily the last step in thinking or problem solving. It is quite possible that the evaluation process will in some cases be the prelude to the acquisition of new knowledge, a new attempt at comprehension or application, or a new analysis and synthesis. (p. 185)

In summary, the hierarchical structure of Bloom's Taxonomy simply did not hold together well from logical or empirical perspectives. As Rohwer and Sloane (1994) note, "The structure claimed for the hierarchy, then, *resembles* a hierarchy" (p. 47).

Toward a New Taxonomy

Recognizing the incredible contribution of Bloom's Taxonomy, this work seeks to outline the design of a New Taxonomy of educational objectives—one that incorporates the best of what Bloom's work has to offer with what has been learned over the 40 plus years since Bloom's Taxonomy was published. The rationale for and the applications of the New Taxonomy, as it is referred to throughout this text, is presented in the next five chapters. However, as the title of this volume indicates, the author acknowledges that this is only a beginning step in the development of a framework that can truly add to that developed by Bloom and his colleagues.

Summary

This chapter has presented a brief discussion of the nature and impact of Bloom's Taxonomy. It has highlighted the problems inherent in its structure while recognizing the strength of its contribution.

CHAPTER 2

A Theoretical Model

One of the problems in the approach taken by Bloom and his colleagues is that it attempted to use degrees of difficulty as the basis of the differences between levels of the taxonomy. Evaluation activities were assumed to be more difficult than activities that involved syntheses, which were assumed to be more difficult than activities involving analysis, and so on. Ultimately, any attempt to design a taxonomy based on difficulty of mental processing is doomed to failure. This occurs because of the well-established principle in psychology that even the most complex of processes can be learned at the level at which it is performed with little or no conscious effort (for discussions, see Anderson, 1983, 1990b, 1995; LaBerge, 1995; LaBerge & Samuels, 1974). The difficulty of a mental process is a function of at least two factors—the inherent complexity of the process in terms of steps involved and the level of familiarity one has with the process. The complexity of a mental process is invariant—the number of steps and their relationship do not change. However, familiarity with a process will change over time. The more familiar one is with a process, the more quickly one executes it and the easier it becomes.

Although mental processes cannot be ordered hierarchically in terms of difficulty, they can be ordered in terms of control—some processes exercise control over the operation of other processes. The model used to develop the New Taxonomy as described in this book is presented in Figure 2.1.

The model depicted in Figure 2.1 not only describes how human beings decide whether to engage in a new task at some point in time, but it also explains how information is processed once a decision to engage has been made. The model presents three mental systems—the self-system, the metacognitive system, and the cognitive system. The fourth component of the model is knowledge.

In this theory, a "new task" is defined as an opportunity to change whatever one is doing or attending to at a particular time. For example, assume that Lisa is in a science class, daydreaming about an upcoming social activity after school. At that moment, her energy and attention are on the social activity. However, if her teacher asked her to pay attention to some new information that was being presented about science, she would be confronted with a decision regarding a new task. The decision Lisa would make and her subsequent

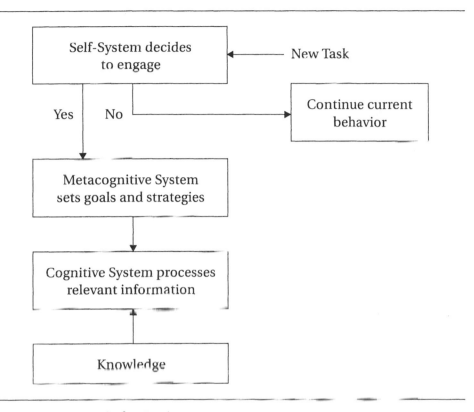

Figure 2.1. Model of Behavior

actions would be determined by the interaction of her self-, her metacognitive, and her cognitive systems, as well as her knowledge. Specifically, the self-system is engaged first, then the metacognitive system, and finally the cognitive system. All three systems use the student's store of knowledge.

The Three Systems and Knowledge

The self-system contains a network of interrelated beliefs and goals (Harter, 1980; Markus & Ruvulo, 1990) that are used to make judgments about the advisability of engaging in a new task. The self-system is also a prime determiner in the motivation one brings to a task (Garcia & Pintrich, 1991, 1993, 1995; Pintrich & Garcia, 1992). If a task is judged important, if the probability of success is high, and positive affect is generated or associated with the task, the individual will be motivated to engage in the new task (Ajzen, 1985; Ajzen & Fishbein, 1977, 1980; Ajzen & Madden, 1986). If the new task is evaluated as having low relevance and/or low probability of success and has an associated negative affect, motivation to engage in the task is low. To be motivated to attend to the new science information, then, Lisa would have to perceive the information as more important than the social event, believe she can comprehend the information, and have no strong negative emotions associated with it.

If a new task is selected, the metacognitive system is engaged. One of the initial jobs of the metacognitive system is to set goals relative to the new task (Schank & Abelson, 1977). This system is also responsible for designing strategies for accomplishing a given goal once it has been set (Sternberg, 1977, 1984a, 1984b, 1986a, 1986b). In terms of the student in the science class, the metacognitive system would be responsible for setting learning goals relative to the new information and designing strategies to accomplish those goals. The metacognitive system, once engaged, is continually interacting with the cognitive system.

The cognitive system is responsible for the effective processing of the information that is essential to the completion of a task. It is responsible for analytic operations such as making inference, comparing, classifying, and the like. For example, as Lisa listens to the new information, she would undoubtedly have to make inferences about it, compare it with what she already knows, and so on.

Finally, relative to any new task, success is highly dependent on the amount of knowledge an individual has about that task (Anderson, 1995; Lindsay & Norman, 1977). For example, the extent to which the science student achieves her learning goals would to a great extent depend on her prior knowledge about the science topic.

The Model and Bloom's Taxonomy

How, then, does the model depicted in Figure 2.1 improve on Bloom's efforts? It does so in at least two ways. First, it presents a model or a "theory" of human thought as opposed to a "framework." Technically, models and theories are systems that allow one to predict phenomena; frameworks are loosely organized sets of principles that describe characteristics of a given phenomenon, but do not necessarily allow for the prediction of phenomena. (For a discussion of models, theories, and frameworks, see Anderson, 1990a.) By definition, Bloom's Taxonomy is a framework in that it describes six general categories of information processing. They are certainly useful categories in helping educators understand the multifaceted nature of learning. Indeed, in his 1977 edition of *Conditions of Learning*, Robert Gagne commented on the "ingenious" contributions of the authors of the taxonomy to an understanding of the various categories of learning. However, Bloom's Taxonomy was not designed to predict specific behaviors (Rohwer & Sloane, 1994) and is, therefore, not a model or theory. The depiction in Figure 2.1 allows for the prediction of specific behaviors within specific situations. For example, given an understanding of an individual's beliefs within the self-system, one can predict the attention that will be paid to a given task and the motivation that will be displayed.

Second (and more important relative to the discussion), the theory presented here improves on Bloom's effort in that it allows for the design of a hierarchical system of human thought from the perspective of two criteria: (1) flow of information and (2) level of consciousness. Here we briefly consider the criterion of flow of information. The criterion of level of consciousness is discussed at the end of Chapter 4, where the details of the New Taxonomy are articulated.

In terms of flow of information, processing always starts with the self-system, proceeds to the metacognitive system, then to the cognitive system, and finally to the knowledge domains. In addition, the status of the various factors within one system affects the status of the various factors within lower systems. For example, if the self-system contains no beliefs that would render a given task important, the individual will either not engage in the task or will engage with low motivation. If the task is deemed important, but a clear goal is not established by the metacognitive system, execution of the task will break down. If clear goals have been established and effectively monitored, but the information processing functions within the cognitive system do not operate effectively, the task will not be carried out. The three systems, then, represent a true hierarchy in terms of flow of processing.

Some Empirical Evidence

Although the New Taxonomy as described in this volume and the theory on which it is built are presented only as a starting place, some data have been collected affirming the hierarchical relationship among the three systems. Specifically, in a recent meta-analysis involving over 2,500 effect sizes, instructional strategies were analyzed as to which of the three systems they used (see Marzano, 1998). For example, if an instructional strategy addressed student beliefs and attitudes, it was coded as employing the self-system. If an instructional technique addressed the establishment of instructional goals, it was coded as employing the metacognitive system. Finally, if the instructional technique addressed the analysis of information, it was coded as employing the cognitive system. The findings of the meta-analysis are reported in Figure 2.2.

As indicated in Figure 2.2, the average effect size for instructional strategies that use the cognitive system is .55, indicating that these instructional techniques produce a gain of 21 percentile points on the average in terms of

System	ES	n	Percentile Gain
Self-System	.74	147	27
Metacognitive System	.72	556	26
Cognitive System	.55	1772	21

Figure 2.2. Meta-Analysis of Instructional Strategies: Effects of Three Systems of Thought on Knowledge Gain

NOTE: ES = effect size; n = number of effect sizes

students' understanding and use of knowledge. The average effect size for instructional techniques that employ the metacognitive system is .72, signaling an achievement gain of 26 percentile points. The average effect size for instructional techniques that employ the self-system is .74, indicating an achievement gain of 27 percentile points. This is the largest of the three. At least, as indicated in this study, the self-system exerts more influence over learning than does the metacognitive system, which, in turn, exerts more influence over learning than does the cognitive system.

Again, it is premature to ascertain the validity of the structure of the New Taxonomy or the theory on which it is built. However, the results of the meta-analysis provide some preliminary evidence that the relationship among the three systems might be hierarchical as depicted.

Summary

In this chapter a model was presented that forms the basis of the New Taxonomy. It describes three systems of thought that have a hierarchical relationship—the self-system, the metacognitive system, and the cognitive system.

CHAPTER 3

The Knowledge Domains

One of the defining differences between Bloom's Taxonomy and the New Taxonomy is that the New Taxonomy separates various types of knowledge from the mental processes that operate on them. This is depicted in Figure 3.1.

As described in Chapter 1, on the one hand, Bloom defined the knowledge category within his Taxonomy as the cognitive operations of recall or recognition.

> By knowledge, we mean that the student can give evidence that he remembers either by recalling or by recognizing some idea or phenomenon with which he has had experience in the educational process. For our taxonomy purposes, we are defining knowledge as little more than the remembering of the idea or phenomenon in a form very close to that in which it was originally encountered. (1956, pp. 28-29)

On the other hand, Bloom identified specific types of knowledge within the knowledge category. These included

Terminology

Specific facts

Conventions

Trends or sequences

Classifications and categories

Criteria

Methodology

Principles and generalizations

Theories and structures

This mixing of types of knowledge with the various mental operations that act on knowledge is one of the major weaknesses of Bloom's Taxonomy since,

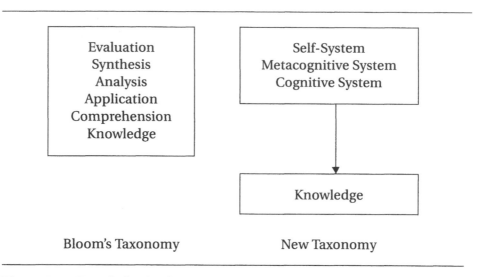

Figure 3.1. Knowledge in the Two Taxonomies

by definition, it confuses the object of an action with the action itself. In somewhat of a self-accusatory manner, Bloom noted that there was a fundamental difference between his knowledge category and the other five levels. Specifically, Bloom separated the knowledge category from the other five levels by a detailed discussion of "intellectual abilities and skills" (pp. 38, 39). Thus, Bloom implicitly recognized the difference between knowledge and the mental operations that are executed on knowledge, but he mixed the two in the basic structure of his taxonomy.

The New Taxonomy avoids this confusion by postulating three domains of knowledge that are operated on by the three systems of thought and their component elements. It is the systems of thought that have the hierarchical structure that constitutes the New Taxonomy. As described in Chapter 5, these hierarchical mental operations interact differentially with the three knowledge domains. In this chapter we consider the knowledge domains.

Knowledge as Domains

Knowledge plays a key role in one's ability to successfully engage in a new task. Without the necessary knowledge, a student can be highly motivated to engage in the task (self-system thinking), set specific goals relative to the task (metacognitive thinking), and even bring to bear a series of keen, analytic skills (cognitive thinking). However, unless the student possesses the requisite knowledge for the task, the effects of these mental processes will be minimal.

Knowledge can be organized into three general categories: information, mental procedures, and psychomotor procedures. Any subject area can be described in terms of how much of these three types of knowledge it comprises. For example, the knowledge specific to the subject of geography includes information about various locations, weather patterns, and the influences that location has on the development of a region; the knowledge associated with geography also includes mental procedures such as how to read and use a contour map or how to read and use a political map. There is probably little, if any, psychomotor knowledge that is specific to geography. Flying an airplane, on the other hand, requires a significant amount of psychomotor knowledge. For example, a pilot must master the physical skills involved in such activities as landing and taking off. Informational knowledge necessary to be an effective pilot would include an understanding of certain concepts such as lift and drag. Finally, the mental procedure knowledge necessary to be an effective pilot would include strategies for efficient scanning and interpreting an instrument panel.

Given the inherent differences in these types of knowledge, it is useful to think of them as related *domains* that are acted upon by the cognitive, metacognitive, and self-systems.

The Domain of Information

The domain of information, sometimes referred to as declarative knowledge, can be conceptualized as hierarchic in its own right. At the bottom of the informational hierarchy are "vocabulary terms." A vocabulary term is a word or phrase about which a student has an accurate, but not necessarily a deep, level of understanding. For example, a student might have a general understanding of the term, *probability,* but not know all the nuances of the various applications of probability. This is not to say that knowledge of vocabulary is unimportant. Indeed, it is fairly obvious that students must understand a certain amount of the basic vocabulary in a subject area before they can understand the facts, generalizations, and concepts within a content area. This might explain why teachers frequently must devote a significant amount of time to vocabulary instruction. For example, after analyzing popular textbooks, Bloom (1976) concluded that textbooks commonly introduce as many as 100 to 150 new terms per chapter (p. 25).

At a level above vocabulary items are facts. Facts present information about specific persons, places, things, and events. To illustrate, "The Battle of Gettysburg was pivotal to the outcome of the Civil War" is a fact. To understand this fact, a student must understand the words (i.e., vocabulary terms), *pivotal,* and *outcome.* At the top of the hierarchy are more general structures such as generalizations and principles. The statement, "Specific battles some-times disproportionately influence the outcome of a war," is a generalization. Although vocabulary terms and facts are important, generalizations help students develop a broad knowledge base because they transfer more readily to different situations. For instance, the preceding generalization can be applied to countries, situations, and ages, whereas the fact of the Battle of Gettysburg is a specific event that does not transfer directly to other situations. This is not to say that facts are unimportant. On the contrary, to truly understand generalizations, students must be able to support them with exemplifying facts. For example, to understand the generalization about the influences of specific battles, students need a rich set of illustrative facts, one of which is probably that regarding the Battle of Gettysburg.

The various types of knowledge within the information domain are described in more detail in Figure 3.2.

Those familiar with the literature on types of information might notice that Figure 3.2 does not list "concepts," although they are frequently listed in other discussions. This is because concepts, as described by other theorists, are basically synonymous with generalizations as described in this work. To illustrate, Gagne describes a concept as "a particular kind of rule, a rule that classifies" (1977, p. 134). As described in Figure 3.2, this is a defining feature of generalizations. Concepts, then, as discussed in other works, are basically identical with what is defined as a generalization or principle in the New Taxonomy.

Although there are many components in the informational domain, ranging from vocabulary terms to different types of principles, it is appropriate and useful for the purpose of the New Taxonomy to organize the types of information into two broad categories: details and organizing ideas. Details include vocabulary terms, facts, time sequences, cause/effect sequences and episodes; organizing ideas include generalizations and principles. This is depicted as follows:

Details
    Episodes
    Cause/effect sequences
    Time sequences
    Facts
    Vocabulary terms

Organizing ideas
    Principles
    Generalizations

As demonstrated in Chapter 5, the three systems of thought—cognitive, meta-cognitive, and self-systems—interact in the same way within these two cate-

(text continues on page 22)

Vocabulary Terms

At the most specific level of informational knowledge are vocabulary terms. In this system, knowing a vocabulary term means understanding the meaning of a word at a very general level. For example, when a student understands declarative knowledge at the level of a vocabulary term, he or she has a general idea what the word means and no serious misconceptions about its meaning. To organize classroom content as vocabulary terms is to organize it as independent words. The expectation is that students have an accurate, but somewhat surface-level, understanding of the meaning of these terms.

Facts

Facts are a very specific type of informational content. Facts convey information about specific persons, places, living and nonliving things, and events. They commonly articulate information such as the following:

- The characteristics of a specific person (e.g., The fictitious character Robin Hood first appeared in English literature in the early 1800s)
- The characteristics of a specific place (e.g., Denver is in the state of Colorado)
- The characteristics of specific living and nonliving things (e.g., My dog, Tuffy, is a golden retriever. The Empire State Building is over 100 stories high.)
- The characteristics of a specific event (e.g., Construction began on the Leaning Tower of Pisa in 1174)

Time Sequences

Time sequences include important events that occurred between two points in time. For example, the events that occurred between President Kennedy's assassination on November 22, 1963, and his burial on November 25, 1963, are organized as a time sequence in most people's memories. First one thing happened, then another, then another.

Cause/Effect Sequences

Cause/effect sequences involve events that produce a product or an effect. A causal sequence can be as simple as a single cause for a single effect. For example, the fact that the game was lost because a certain player dropped the ball in the end zone can be organized as a causal sequence. More commonly, however, effects have complex networks of causes; one event affects another

Figure 3.2. Types of Informational Knowledge *(continued)*

that combines with a third event to affect a fourth that then affects another, and so on. For example, the events leading up to the Civil War can be organized as a causal sequence.

Episodes

Episodes are specific events that have (a) a setting (e.g., a particular time and place), (b) specific participants, (c) a particular duration, (d) a specific sequence of events, and (e) a particular cause and effect. For example, the events of Watergate could be organized as an episode: The episode occurred at a particular time and place; it had specific participants; it lasted for a specific duration of time; it involved a specific sequence of events; it was caused by specific events; and it had a specific effect on the country.

Generalizations

Generalizations are statements for which examples can be provided. For example, the statement, "U.S. presidents often come from families that have great wealth or influence," is a generalization, for which examples can be provided. It is easy to confuse some generalizations with some facts. Facts identify characteristics of *specific* persons, places, living and nonliving things, and events, whereas generalizations identify characteristics about *classes* or *categories* of persons, places, living and nonliving things, and events. For example, the statement, "My dog, Tuffy, is a golden retriever" is a fact. However, the statement, "Golden retrievers are good hunters," is a generalization. In addition, generalizations identify characteristics about abstractions. Specifically, information about abstractions is always stated in the form of generalizations. The following are examples of the various types of generalizations:

- Characteristics of classes of persons (e.g., It takes at least two years of training to become a fireman.)
- Characteristics of classes of places (e.g., Large cities have high crime rates.)
- Characteristics of classes of living and nonliving things (e.g., Golden retrievers are good hunting dogs. Firearms are the subject of great debate.)
- Characteristics of classes of events (e.g., The Super Bowl is the premier sporting event each year.)
- Characteristics of abstractions (e.g., Love is one of the most powerful human emotions.)

Figure 3.2. Continued

Principles

Principles are specific types of generalizations that deal with relationships. In general, there are two types of principles found in school-related declarative knowledge: *cause/effect principles* and *correlational principles.*

Cause/effect principles. Cause/effect principles articulate causal relationships. For example, the sentence, "Tuberculosis is caused by the tubercle bacillus," is a cause/effect principle. Although not stated here, understanding a cause/effect principle includes knowledge of the specific elements within the cause/effect system and the exact relationships those elements have to one another. That is, to understand the cause/effect principle regarding tuberculosis and the bacterium, one would have to understand the sequence of events that occur, the elements involved, and the type and strength of relationships between those elements. In short, understanding a cause/effect principle involves a great deal of information.

Correlational principles. Correlational principles describe relationships that are not necessarily causal in nature, but in which a change in one factor is associated with a change in another factor. For example, the following is a correlational principle: "The increase in lung cancer among women is directly proportional to the increase in the number of women who smoke."

Again, to understand this principle, a student would have to know the specific details about this relationship. Specifically, a student would have to know the general pattern of this relationship, that is, the number of women who have lung cancer changes at the same rate as the number of women who smoke changes.

These two types of principles are sometimes confused with cause/effect *sequences.* A cause/effect sequence applies to a specific situation, whereas a principle applies to many situations. The causes of the Civil War taken together represent a cause/effect sequence. They apply to the Civil War only. However, the cause/effect principle linking tuberculosis and the tubercle bacillus can be applied to many different situations and many different people. Physicians use this principle to make judgments about a variety of situations and a variety of people. The key distinction between principles and cause/effect sequences is that principles can be exemplified in a number of situations, whereas cause/effect sequences cannot—they apply to a single situation only.

Figure 3.2. Continued

SOURCE: Adapted from Marzano & Kendall, 1996a, *A Comprehensive Guide to Designing Standards-Based Districts, Schools, and Classrooms.* Reprinted with permission.

1. Max walks.
2. Max is handsome.
3. Max eats fruit.
4. Max is in London.
5. Max gave a toy to Molly.
6. Max walks slowly.
7. Max hit Bill with a pillow.
8. Sorrow overcame Max.

Figure 3.3. Major Types of Propositions

gories, but somewhat differently between categories. That is, the processes within the cognitive system apply to episodes in the same way that they apply to facts. Similarly, the processes within the cognitive system apply to principles in the same way they apply to generalizations. However, the processes within the cognitive system do not apply to generalizations the same way they apply to episodes.

A final characteristic of informational knowledge important to a discussion of the New Taxonomy is the manner in which it is represented in memory. Some psychologists assert that informational knowledge exists in propositional form in memory. The construct of a proposition has a rich history in both psychology and linguistics (Frederiksen, 1975; Kintsch, 1974; Norman & Rumelhart, 1975). In simple terms, "a proposition is the smallest unit of thought that can stand as a separate assertion, that is, the smallest unit about which it makes sense to make the judgment true or false" (Anderson, 1990b, p.123). Clark and Clark (1977) have noted that there is a finite set of the types of propositions. Figure 3.3 depicts the major types of propositions.

Each of the statements in Figure 3.3 can be affirmed or denied, yet none of their component parts can. That is, one could determine if it is true that Max walks or Max is handsome, but one could not confirm or deny *Max, walks, is,* or *handsome* in isolation. Propositions, then, might be described as the most basic form in which information is stored.

Propositions are combined in propositional networks to form complex information. For example, Figure 3.4 represents the propositional network for the statements: "Bill went to the drugstore where he met his sister. They bought their father a coat."

Note that the lines in Figure 3.4 are labeled *agent, object, locative,* and *receiver.* These represent the various types of relationships that can exist between propositions and between the elements within propositions. (For discussions of the types of relationships in propositional networks, see Chafe, 1970; Fillmore, 1968; Turner & Greene, 1977.)

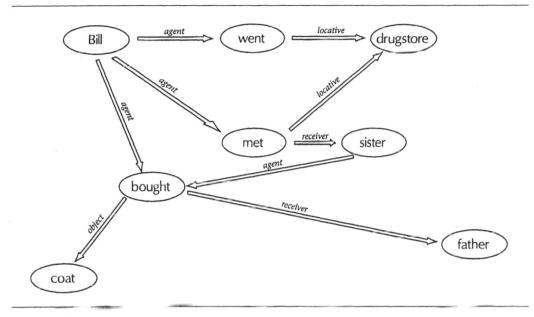

Figure 3.4. Propositional Network

The Domain of Mental Procedures

Mental procedures—sometimes referred to as procedural knowledge—are different in form and function from information or declarative knowledge. The distinction between declarative/procedural knowledge is considered basic by some psychologists. For example, psychologists Snow and Lohman (1989) note that "the distinction between declarative and procedural knowledge, or more simply, content knowledge and process knowledge" is one of the most basic in terms of guiding educational practice (p. 266).

Whereas declarative knowledge can be considered the "what" of human knowledge, procedural knowledge can be described as the "how-to." For example, an individual's knowledge about how to drive a car or how to do long division is procedural in nature. Again, the format in which procedures are stored in memory is highly relevant to the discussion of the New Taxonomy.

Psychologist John Anderson (1983) has described the basic nature of procedural knowledge as "IF-THEN" structures called productions. The structure of productions is different from the structure of propositional networks—the basic format of informational knowledge. To illustrate, the following is part of the production network for the procedure of multicolumn subtraction:

1a. IF the goal is to do multicolumn subtraction,

1b. THEN make the goal to process the right-most column.

2a. IF there is an answer in the current column and there is a column to the left,

2b. THEN make the goal to process the column to the left.

3a. IF the goal is to process a column and there is no bottom digit or the bottom digit is zero,

3b. THEN record the top digit as the answer, and so on.

In its entirety, this production network would have scores of IF/THEN pairs—scores of productions. (For a complete discussion of production networks, see Anderson, 1983, 1990a, 1990b, 1995.) Knowledge within the domain of mental procedures, then, is different in structure from knowledge within the domain of information.

Another important feature of knowledge in the domain of mental procedures as it relates to the New Taxonomy is the manner in which it is learned. Specifically, there are three relatively distinct phases to the acquisition of mental procedures. Fitts (1964) calls the first stage the "cognitive" stage. At this stage, the learner can verbalize the process (describe it, if asked) and might be able to perform at least a crude approximation of the procedure. According to Anderson (1983), at this stage it is common to observe verbal "mediation" during which the learner rehearses the information required to execute the skill. In the second stage, called the "associative" stage by Fitts, the performance of the procedure is smoothed out. At this stage errors in the initial understanding of the procedure are detected and deleted along with the need for verbal rehearsal. During the third stage, the "autonomous" stage, the procedure is refined. It is at this level that the procedure becomes automatic (LaBerge & Samuels, 1974). That is, the procedure once called on by the learner is automatically executed and takes very little of the available space in working memory.

These phases of acquisition are important to the New Taxonomy because procedural knowledge acquired at the first stage only—Fitts's cognitive stage—is, for all practical purposes, identical with information knowledge. To illustrate, at the first stage of learning multicolumn subtraction, Jim might be able to describe the procedure and even answer questions about it, but he might not actually be able to perform it. Thus, even though the procedure has a production structure, it is understood by learners in the same way they would understand informational knowledge. As we shall see in Chapter 5, this characteristic of procedural knowledge has implications for how it is acted upon by the various levels of the New Taxonomy.

Like the domain of information, the domain of mental procedures can be organized into a simple hierarchy. At the top of the hierarchy are highly robust procedures that have a diversity of possible products or outcomes and involve the execution of many interrelated subprocedures. Technically, such operations are referred to as *macroprocedures* (Marzano & Kendall, 1996a). The prefix *macro* indicates that the procedure is highly complex, having many subcomponents that require some form of management. For example, the procedure of writing fulfills the defining characteristics of a macroprocedure. Different students writing on the same topic will produce very different compositions even though they are addressing the same topic and executing the same steps.

Somewhat in the middle of the hierarchy are mental procedures that do not generate the variety of products possible from macroprocedures and do not incorporate the wide variety of subcomponents. These procedures are commonly referred to as tactics (see Snowman & McCown, 1984). For example, an individual may have a tactic for reading a histogram. Tactics do not consist of a set of steps that must be performed in a specific order. Rather, they are made up of general rules with an overall flow of execution. For example, a tactic for reading a histogram might include rules that address (a) identifying the elements depicted in the legend, (b) determining what is reported in each axis on the graph, and (c) determining the relationship between the elements on the two axes. Although there is a general pattern in which these rules are executed, there is no rigid or set order.

Algorithms are mental procedures that normally do not vary in application. They have very specific outcomes and very specific steps. The previous example of multicolumn subtraction is an illustration of an algorithm. Algorithms must be learned to the level of automaticity to be useful.

The simplest type of mental procedure is a *single rule*, or a small set of rules with no accompanying steps. A single rule would consist of one IF/THEN production—IF situation *X* occurs, THEN perform action *Y.* Single-rule mental procedures are commonly employed in sets. For example, a student who knows five rules for capitalization might apply these independently while editing his or her writing. In such a situation, the student would be using a group of single-rule procedures. If the student systematically executed the rules in a set sequence, however (e.g., check capitalization at the beginning of each sentence first, next check the capitalization of proper nouns, and so on), the student would have organized the single-rule procedures into a tactic or algorithm, depending on how rigidly the pattern of execution was followed.

For the purpose of the New Taxonomy, it is useful to organize the domain of mental procedures into two broad categories: those that, with practice, can be executed automatically or with little conscious thought, and those that must be controlled. Tactics, algorithms, and single rules can be learned to the level of automaticity or to the level of little conscious thought. Macroprocedures, by definition, require controlled execution. As a set, tactics, algorithms, and single rules will be referred to as skills; macroprocedures will be referred to simply as processes. Thus, as the following depicts, the two categories of mental procedures within the New Taxonomy are processes and skills:

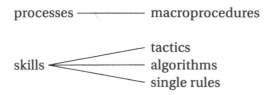

processes ———————— macroprocedures

skills <   tactics
                        algorithms
                        single rules

The Domain of Psychomotor Procedures

As the name implies, the psychomotor domain is composed of physical procedures an individual uses to negotiate daily life and to engage in complex physical activities for work and for recreation. It should be noted that Bloom and his colleagues (Bloom et al., 1956) originally intended to address psychomotor skills as a separate domain. However, the document describing this domain was never published. A fair question, then, is, Why is the psychomotor domain considered a type of knowledge in the New Taxonomy?

Psychomotor procedures are considered a type of knowledge for two reasons. First, psychomotor procedures are stored in memory in a fashion identical with mental procedures. They are stored as IF/THEN production networks (Anderson, 1983). Second, the stages of development for acquiring psychomotor procedures are similar to, if not identical with, those involved in acquiring mental procedures (Anderson, 1983, 1995; Gagne, 1977, 1989). That is, they are first learned as information; during initial practice they are shaped, then finally learned to a level of automaticity or near automaticity.

As is the case with the other two domains, the psychomotor domain can be organized into a hierarchy. At the bottom of the psychomotor hierarchy are foundational physical abilities upon which more complex procedures are developed. Carroll (1993) has identified a number of these foundational abilities, which include

- Static strength
- Overall body equilibrium
- Speed of limb movement
- Wrist-finger speed

- Finger dexterity
- Manual dexterity
- Arm-hand steadiness
- Control precision

It is clear from this listing that these procedures are generally developed without formal instruction. Indeed, human beings perform all these physical functions naturally with a certain degree of acumen. However, this is not to say that these foundational skills cannot be improved with instruction and practice. For example, with instruction, a person's manual dexterity can be improved. Therefore, they qualify as types of knowledge in that they can be learned.

At a level up from basic foundational procedures are simple combination procedures such as shooting a free throw in basketball. As their name implies, simple combination procedures involve sets of foundational procedures acting in parallel. For example, shooting a free throw is an example of a simple combination procedure that involves the interaction of a number of foundational procedures, such as wrist-finger speed, control precision, and arm-hand steadiness.

Finally, complex combination procedures use sets of simple combination procedures. For example, the act of playing defense in basketball would involve the combination skills of side-to-side movement with the body in a squatting position, hand waving, and so on. Thus, what is commonly thought of as a sport or a recreational activity can be operationally defined as the use of a set of complex combination procedures for the purpose of accomplishing specific physical goals (e.g., hitting a ball over a net within prescribed boundaries while using a specific type of racquet).

Again, for purposes of the New Taxonomy, it is useful to organize the procedures in the psychomotor domain into two categories:

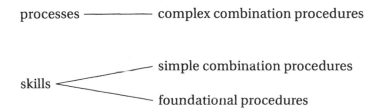

In summary, for the purposes of the New Taxonomy, the components in the three domains of knowledge have been organized as depicted in Figure 3.5.

Information	1. organizing ideas	principles generalizations
	2. details	episodes cause/effect sequences time sequences facts vocabulary terms
Mental Procedures	1. processes 2. skills	macro procedures tactics algorithms single rules
Psychomotor Procedures	1. processes 2. skills	complex combination procedures simple combination procedures foundational procedures

Figure 3.5. Components of the Three Knowledge Domains

Relationship to Bloom's Taxonomy

As described at the beginning of this chapter, the convention employed in the New Taxonomy of considering knowledge as that which is acted upon by various mental processes is a significant departure from Bloom's Taxonomy. Another significant difference is the New Taxonomy's inclusion of psychomotor procedures as a type of knowledge akin to mental procedures and information. One similarity, however, between the New Taxonomy and Bloom's Taxonomy is their respective delineation of informational types. Both place terms and phrases at the lower end of the information hierarchy, and generalizations and principles at the higher end.

Summary

This chapter has described three domains of knowledge: (1) information, (2) mental procedures, and (3) psychomotor procedures. Whereas information is stored as propositional networks, mental and psychomotor procedures are stored as production networks. The components within each of the three domains were organized into two categories. The informational domain was subdivided into details and organizing ideas. The domains of mental procedures and psychomotor procedures were organized into skills and processes.

CHAPTER 4

The Three Systems of Thinking

The three systems of thought introduced in Chapter 2 are at the heart of the New Taxonomy. As we have seen, these three systems—the self-system, the metacognitive system, and the cognitive system—can be ordered hierarchically. In addition, as will be explained at the end of this chapter, the four elements of the cognitive system can be ordered hierarchically. This makes for a six-tiered taxonomy as depicted in Figure 4.1, which represents the basic structure of the New Taxonomy. Each of the six levels is described in this chapter. However, to be able to discuss these six levels in detail, it is necessary to consider briefly the nature and function of memory.

Memory

There have been many models proposed for the nature and function of human memory. Anderson (1995) explains that the long-held conception of two types of memory—short-term and long-term—has been replaced with the theory that there is only one type of memory, with different functions. For the purpose of this discussion, we consider three functions: sensory memory, permanent memory, and working memory.

Sensory memory deals with the temporary storage of data from the senses. Anderson describes sensory memory in the following way:

> Sensory memory is capable of storing more or less complete records of what has been encountered for brief periods of time, during which people can note relationships among the elements and encode the elements in a more permanent memory. If the information in sensory memory is not encoded in the brief time before it decays, it is lost. What subjects encode depends on what they are paying attention to. The environment typically offers much more information at one time than we can attend to and encode. Therefore, much of what enters our sensory system results in no permanent record. (1995, p. 160)

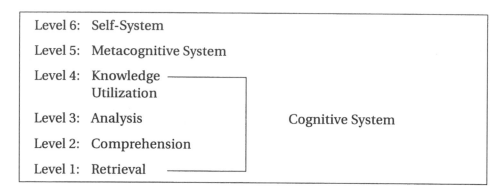

Figure 4.1. Six Levels of the New Taxonomy

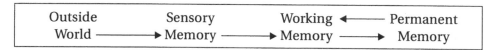

Figure 4.2. Types of Memory

Permanent memory contains all information, organizing ideas, skills, and processes that constitute the domains of knowledge. In short, all that we understand and know how to do is stored in permanent memory.

Working memory uses data from both sensory memory and permanent memory. As its name implies, working memory is where data are actively processed. This is depicted in Figure 4.2.

As depicted in Figure 4.2, working memory can receive data from sensory memory (where it is held only briefly), from permanent memory (where it resides permanently), or from both. There is no theoretical limit on the amount of time data can reside in working memory. As long as an individual focuses conscious attention on the data in working memory, it stays active. To this extent, working memory can be considered the "seat of consciousness." That is, our experience of consciousness is actually our experience of what is being processed in working memory (Dennett, 1969, 1991).

Level 1: Retrieval (Cognitive System)

Having a basic understanding of the construct of working memory, we can describe retrieval as the activation and transfer of knowledge from permanent memory to working memory, where it might be consciously processed. Retrieval is a process within the cognitive system and is, of course, an innate process—it is part of every human's neurological "hard-wiring." It is generally done without conscious awareness by an individual.

The actual process involved in retrieval is somewhat different, depending on the type of knowledge that is retrieved. In terms of the domain of information, retrieval involves the simple transfer of details or organizing ideas from permanent memory into working memory. In the New Taxonomy, this type of retrieval is referred to as recall. For example, when a student retrieves information about the 1999 conflict in Kosovo from permanent memory and deposits it in working memory, it involves recalling a detail from the information domain. When a student retrieves information about Bernoulli's principle and deposits it in working memory, it involves recalling an organizing idea.

It is important to note that when information is retrieved from permanent memory, it most probably contains components that were not explicit in the student's initial experience with the information, because human beings naturally elaborate on information as initially taken into working memory. To illustrate, assume that an individual hears the following information as a part of a discussion with someone:

> The two young girls, Mary and Sally, saw the book of matches and immediately began thinking of games to play. By midafternoon the house was engulfed in flames.

In a strictly logical sense, this information is incomplete. There is no statement as to the direct relationship between the games the children played and the fire. To make sense of what was explicitly stated, an individual would necessarily infer missing information, such as: The children began playing with the matches; their game caught the house on fire. In working memory, the implicit information would be enhanced to produce a coherent whole like the following:

Proposition 1: The two young girls, Mary and Sally, saw the matches (stated).

Proposition 2: The children began thinking of games (stated).

Proposition 3: The games included using the matches (inferred).

Proposition 4: While the children were playing games with the matches, the house caught on fire (inferred).

Proposition 5: The fire was accidental (inferred).

Proposition 6: The house caught on fire in the early afternoon (inferred).

Proposition 7: By midafternoon the house was engulfed in flames (stated).

Proposition 8: The house was destroyed or severely damaged (inferred).

Some researchers have referred to this more logically complete version of the information as a "microstructure" (Turner & Greene, 1977). Obviously, inference plays a major role in the design of a complete microstructure. There are two basic types of inferences an individual makes when constructing a microstructure: default inferences and reasoned inferences. Default inferences are those you commonly make about people, places, things, events, and abstractions (de Beaugrande, 1980; Kintsch, 1979; van Dijk, 1980). For example, when you read the sentence, "Bill had a dog," you immediately add information such as "The dog had four legs," "The dog liked to eat bones," "The dog liked to be petted," and so on. In other words, you have information stored about dogs. In the absence of information to the contrary, you infer that this general information you have is true about the dog, even though it is not explicitly mentioned in the text.

Reasoned inferences are another way we add information that is not explicit. Such inferences are not part of our general knowledge. Rather, they are "reasoned conclusions." For example, when you read the statement, "Experimental psychologists believe that you have to test generalizations to see if they are true," and later read about a psychologist who is presented with a new theory by a colleague, you will naturally conclude that the psychologist will probably suggest that the theory be tested. This inference comes not from your general knowledge base about psychologists, but is induced from the earlier information you read about experimental psychologists. In summary, recall of information involves the retrieval from permanent memory of what was explicitly presented when the information was initially encountered, as well as any information that might have been added via default and reasoned inferences.

Although knowledge from the domain of information is only recalled, knowledge from the domains of mental procedures and psychomotor procedures can be *executed* as well as *recalled*. As explained in Chapter 2, procedures of all types have an IF/THEN structure, referred to as productions. When the steps in these productions are carried out, something occurs and a product results. For example, in the case of the production described in the previous chapter regarding multicolumn subtraction, a quantity is computed when the steps are carried out. Thus, we say that procedural knowledge is executed, whereas information is recalled. However, it is also true that procedural knowledge can be recalled, because all procedures have embedded information. To illustrate, reconsider the first part of the production network for the procedure of multicolumn subtraction:

1a.   IF the goal is to do multicolumn subtraction,

1b.   THEN make the goal to process the right-most column.

2a.   IF there is an answer in the current column and there is a column to the left,

2b.   THEN make the goal to process the column to the left.

3a.   IF the goal is to process a column and there is no bottom digit or the bottom digit is zero,

3b.   THEN record the top digit as the answer.

Notice that to execute this procedure effectively, a student would have to understand some basic information, such as

- The number in the right-most column represents ones

- The number in the next column to the left represents tens

- The number in the next column to the left represents hundreds, and so on

Procedures, then, commonly include information that must be understood so that the procedure can be executed effectively. For this reason, procedures—or at least the information embedded within them—can be recalled.

Relationship to Bloom's Taxonomy

As defined in the New Taxonomy, the cognitive process of retrieval is akin to the knowledge level in Bloom's Taxonomy. Again, Bloom described his knowledge category in the following way: "For our taxonomy purposes, we are defining knowledge as little more than remembering the idea or phenomenon in a form very close to that in which it was originally encountered" (pp. 28-29). In addition, Bloom and his colleagues explained that "Knowledge as defined here includes those behaviors and test situations which emphasize the remembering, either by recognition or recall, of ideas, material, or phenomena" (p. 62). Although most of Bloom's examples within his knowledge level deal with information only, one might infer from some of his examples that by knowledge he also means the execution of mental procedures. Again, it is worth noting that Bloom confounded the object of retrieval (i.e., knowledge) with the processes of retrieval (i.e., recall and execution). The New Taxonomy does not.

Level 2: Comprehension (Cognitive System)

The process of comprehension within the cognitive system is responsible for translating knowledge into a form appropriate for storage in permanent memory. That is, data that are deposited in working memory via sensory memory are not stored in permanent memory exactly as experienced. We have seen that the learner quite naturally infers implicit information via default and reasoned inferences. However, to store the information in permanent memory in an efficient manner, it must be translated into a structure and format that preserves the key information, as opposed to extraneous information. The extent to which an individual has stored knowledge in this parsimonious fashion is the extent to which the individual has comprehended that knowledge.

Comprehension, as defined in the New Taxonomy, involves two related processes: synthesis and representation.

Synthesis

Synthesis is the process of distilling knowledge down to its key characteristics, organized in a parsimonious, generalized form—technically referred to as a macrostructure, as opposed to a microstructure (Kintsch, 1974, 1979; van Dijk, 1977, 1980). Whereas the microstructure contains information acquired from direct experience and inference, the macrostructure contains the gist of the information in the microstructure. This synthesis is accomplished via the application of rules technically referred to as *macrorules*. For example, van Dijk and Kintsch (1983) have identified three macrorules that are used to translate a microstructure into a macrostructure:

1. Deletion—given a sequence of propositions, delete any proposition that is not directly related to the other propositions in the sequence.
2. Generalization—replace any proposition by one that includes the information in a more general form.
3. Construction—replace any set of propositions by one or more that include the information in the set stated in more general terms.

When applied appropriately, these rules generate a parsimonious representation of information that does not include all details, but includes the general outline of the critical information. This explains why individuals usually do not remember the specific facts in an interesting story they have read, but do tend to recall the general flow of information and events. To illustrate the product of applying macrorules to the information in the microstructure, reconsider the microstructures about the two children, Mary and Sally, and the fire. The macrostructure for this information might be stated in the following way:

Two children began playing with matches and accidentally started a fire that burned a house down.

Evidence that students have effectively synthesized knowledge is that they can produce the macrostructure for that knowledge—a statement of the important or critical elements of that knowledge.

Representation

Representation is the comprehension process of creating a symbolic analog of the knowledge contained in a macrostructure (which has been produced via the process of synthesis). The concept of representation as a mental process is grounded in dual-coding theories of knowledge such as that articulated by Paivio. According to that theory (Paivio, 1969, 1971) information is processed into two primary modes: a linguistic mode and an imagery mode. The linguistic mode is semantic in nature and, as we have seen, is expressed as propositions or productions. As a metaphor, one might think of the linguistic mode as containing actual statements in permanent memory. The imagery code, in contrast, is expressed as mental pictures or even physical sensations such as smell, taste, touch, kinesthetic association, and sound (Richardson, 1983).

Representation, then, is the translation of the knowledge contained in a macrostructure into some symbolic, imagery (i.e., nonlinguistic) mode. Hayes (1981) provides an example of the representation process, using the following equation from physics:

$$F = \frac{(M_1, M_2)G}{r^2}$$

The equation states that force (F) is equal to the product of the masses of two objects (M_1 and M_2) times a constant (G), divided by the square of the distance between them (r). There are a number of ways this information might be represented symbolically. Hayes (1981) suggests an image of two large globes in space with the learner in the middle trying to hold them apart:

> If either of the globes were very heavy, we would expect that it would be harder to hold them apart than if both were light. Since force increases as either of the masses (M's) increases, the masses must be in the numerator. As we push the globes further apart, the force of attraction between them will decrease as the force of attraction between two magnets decreases as we pull them apart. Since force decreases as distance increases, r must be in the denominator. (p. 127)

A popular form of symbolic representation in K-12 classrooms is graphic organizers, which combine language and symbols. Examples of how graphic organizers can be used across different content areas have been offered by Jones, Palincsar, Ogle, and Carr (1987), Heimlich and Pittelman (1988), McTighe and Lyman (1988), and Clarke (1991). Some assert that most informational knowledge can be symbolized using a very small set of organizational patterns. Combining the work of Cooper (1983), Frederiksen (1977), and Meyer (1975), yields a number of popular organizational patterns like the following:

- *Characteristic patterns* organize facts or characteristics about specific persons, places, things, and events. The characteristics need be in no particular order. For example, information in a film about the state of Colorado—its location, its altitude, specific events that occurred there—might be organized as a simple descriptive pattern.

- *Sequence patterns* organize events in a specific chronological order. For example, a chapter in a book relating the events that occurred during the 1999 war in Kosovo might be organized as a sequence pattern.

- *Process/Cause patterns* organize information into a causal network leading to a specific outcome or into a sequence of steps leading to a specific product. For example, information about the events leading to the war in Kosovo might be organized as a process/cause pattern.

- *Problem/Solution patterns* organize information into an identified problem and its possible solutions. For example, information about the various types of diction errors that might occur in an essay and the ways of correcting those errors might be organized as a problem/solution pattern.

- *Generalization patterns* organize information into a generalization with supporting examples. For example, a chapter in a textbook about U.S. presidents might be organized using this generalization: "U.S. presidents frequently come from influential families." It would be followed by examples of specific presidents.

Each of these patterns lend themselves to a particular type of graphic organizer. These are depicted in Figure 4.3.

Relationship to Bloom's Taxonomy

Comprehension as defined in the New Taxonomy is fairly similar to comprehension as defined in Bloom's Taxonomy. Bloom (1956) describes comprehension in the following way:

Here we are using the term "comprehension" to include those *objectives, behaviors,* or *responses* which represent an understanding of the literal message contained in a communication. In reaching such an understanding, the student may change the communication in his

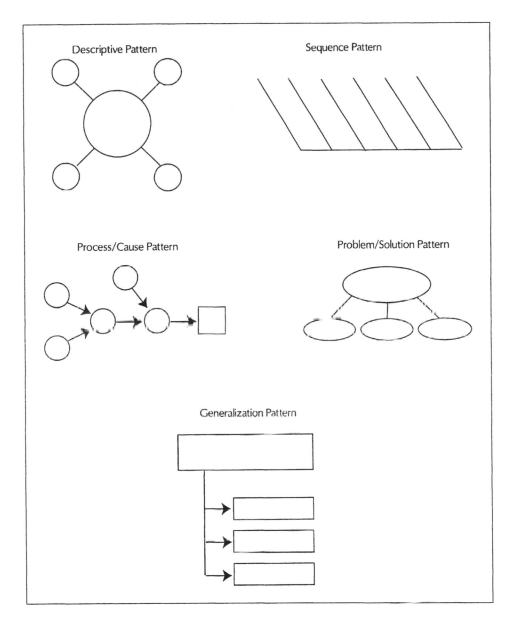

Figure 4.3. Patterns

mind or in his overt responses to some parallel form more meaningful to him. There may also be responses which represent simple extensions beyond what is given in the communication itself. (p. 89)

As discussed, Bloom's Taxonomy identifies three types of comprehension: translation, interpretation, and extrapolation. *Translation* is basically synonymous with representation in the New Taxonomy since both involve encoding knowledge in a form different from that in which it was initially perceived. However, *representation* in the New Taxonomy appears to emphasize symbolic and nonlinguistic forms more than does translation in Bloom's Taxonomy. *Interpretation* in Bloom's Taxonomy appears synonymous with *synthesis* in the New Taxonomy, since both deal with addressing the knowledge as a whole or the gist of the knowledge. *Extrapolation* in Bloom's Taxonomy, however, deals with inferences that appear to go beyond the comprehension processes in the New Taxonomy.

Level 3: Analysis (Cognitive System)

Analysis in the New Taxonomy involves the "reasoned" extension of knowledge. As a function of applying the analysis processes, an individual elaborates on the knowledge as comprehended. These elaborations extend far beyond the "localized" inferences made when knowledge is initially deposited in short-term memory in its microstructure format. Analysis also goes beyond the identification of essential versus nonessential characteristics that are a function of the process of comprehension. Analysis within the New Taxonomy involves the generation of new information not already possessed by the individual.

There are five types of analysis processes: (1) matching, (2) classification, (3) error analysis, (4) generalization, and (5) specification. It should be noted that each of these cognitive operations can be—and frequently are—engaged in naturally without conscious thought. However, when used as analysis tools as defined in the New Taxonomy, they are executed both consciously and rigorously. When applied in this manner, these processes force the learner to cycle through knowledge many times, changing it and refining it.

Many researchers attest to this dynamic of human learning. For example, Piaget (1971) described two basic types of learning: one in which information is integrated into the learner's existing knowledge base, called *assimilation*, and another in which existing knowledge structures are changed, called *accommodation*. Other researchers and theorists have made similar distinctions. For example, Rumelhart and Norman (1981) described three basic types of learning. The first two, called *accretion* and *tuning*, deal with the gradual accumulation or addition of information over time and the expression of that information in more parsimonious ways. The third type of learning, called *restructuring*, involves reorganizing information so that it can produce new insights and be used in new situations. It is this type of learning, described by Piaget as accommodation and by Rumelhart and Norman as restructuring, that is referred to as analysis in the New Taxonomy.

Matching

Matching processes address the identification of similarities and differences between knowledge components. This is perhaps the most basic of all aspects of information processing (Smith & Medin, 1981). That is, matching is fundamental to most, if not all, other types of analysis processes. Researcher Arthur Markman and his colleagues have determined that, of the two aspects of matching, identifying similarities is the more primary, since without the identification of similarities, no differences can be discerned (Gentner & Markman, 1994; Markman & Gentner, 1993a, 1993b; Medin, Goldstone, & Markman, 1995).

The process of matching may be simple or complex, depending on the demands of the task (Mandler, 1983). For example, a young child will easily and naturally notice the similarities between two dogs while walking in the park. However, that child might have difficulty when asked to compare the same two dogs on characteristics that are key features of their respective breeds and explain how these similarities and differences help that breed. It is the latter form of the task that is referred to here as matching.

Stahl (1985) and Beyer (1988) have each developed matching strategies that foster a high degree of analytic thinking. These strategies include the following basic steps:

- Specifying the items to be analyzed
- Specifying the attributes or characteristics on which they are to be analyzed
- Determining how they are alike and different
- Stating similarities and differences as precisely as possible

Classification

Classification refers to organizing knowledge into meaningful categories. Like matching, it is basic to human thought. As Mervis (1980) notes, the world is composed of an infinite number of stimuli. People make the unfamiliar familiar by organizing the myriad stimuli that bombard their senses into like categories. Indeed, Nickerson, Perkins, and Smith (1985) note that the ability to form categories of like stimuli is central to all forms of thought.

Although learners use the process of classification naturally, when used as an analytic tool, this process can be very challenging. Marzano (1992) and others (Beyer, 1988; Jones, Amiran, & Katims, 1985; Taba, 1967) have identified specific steps in the classification process. As defined in the New Taxonomy, classification involves the following components:

- Identify the item to be classified.
- Identify the defining characteristics of that item.

- Identify a superordinate category to which the item belongs and explain why it belongs in that category.

- Identify one or more (if any) subordinate categories for the item and explain how they are related.

As these steps illustrate, to execute the process of classification as defined here, a student must be able to identify knowledge that is superordinate to it and knowledge that is subordinate to it. This goes beyond simply organizing knowledge into like categories (which can be accomplished through simple matching). Classification, as defined in the New Taxonomy, forces the learner to organize knowledge into hierarchic structures.

Error Analysis

The analytic process of error analysis addresses the logic or reasonableness of knowledge. The existence of this cognitive function implies that information must be considered reasonable for an individual to accept it as valid (Gilovich, 1991). To illustrate, assume that Larry is engaged in reading an article on a given topic. As the incoming information is being represented in working memory, he screens the new knowledge to determine if it makes sense relative to what he already knows about the topic. If the information is considered illogical or unreasonable, then it will be either tagged as such prior to being stored in permanent memory, or it will be rejected. Again, people naturally and quickly make judgments regarding how reasonable knowledge is. However, error analysis as an analytic skill within the New Taxonomy involves (a) consciously judging the validity of the knowledge based on explicit criteria and (b) identifying any errors in reasoning that have been presented.

To perform this function well, a student must understand the nature of evidence and well-formed arguments. Toulmin, Rieke, and Janik (1981) have identified the specifics of what students must know to judge validity. This is summarized in Figure 4.4.

Drawing on the work of a number of theorists, Marzano and his colleagues (Marzano et al., 1988; Marzano et al., 1997) have identified a fairly comprehensive list of errors in reasoning that students should understand to effectively analyze incoming information. They are summarized in Figure 4.5.

Generalizing

Generalizing, as defined in the New Taxonomy, is the process of constructing new generalizations from information that is already known. Again, this process involves inference and, again, these inferences go well beyond the inferences made during the creation of a microstructure or a macrostructure.

1. Grounds: Once a claim is made, it is usually supported by grounds. Depending on the type of claim made, grounds may be composed of:
   - Matters of common knowledge
   - Expert opinion
   - Previously established information
   - Experimental observation
   - Other information considered "factual"

   e.g., "Evidence for Hemingway's superiority can be found in reviews of his works by expert literary critic Ralph Johnson."

2. Warrants: Warrants specify or interpret the information in the grounds. That is, where grounds specify the source of support for a claim and the general nature of the support, warrants provide a detailed analysis of the information highlighted by grounds.

   e.g., "In one of Johnson's articles he notes that Hemingway's work exemplifies the first principle of good writing, namely, that it should stir the emotions of the reader."

3. Backing: Backing establishes the validity of warrants. That is, warrants in and of themselves might not be wholly trusted. Consequently, it is often appropriate for there to be some discussion of the validity or general acceptance of the warrants used.

   e.g., "The principle cited by Johnson in his critique of Hemingway is one of the most frequently cited. In fact, Johnson notes that . . ."

4. Qualifiers: Not all warrants lead to their claims with the same degree of certainty. Consequently, qualifiers articulate the degree of certainty for the claim and/or qualifiers to the claim.

   e.g., "It should be noted that Hemingway's expertise is not appreciated by all . . . ."

Figure 4.4. Arguments and Evidence

These inferences are generally considered to be somewhat inductive in nature. Given the inferential nature of generalizing and the common understanding (or misunderstanding) of induction and deduction, it is useful to discuss the two briefly and their relationship to the process of generalizing.

Induction is usually thought of as reasoning from the specific to the general. Holland and his colleagues (Holland, Holyoak, Nisbett, & Thagard, 1986) postulate four types of rules that are the working parts of the induction process. *Specialization rules* state that if a previously generated rule does not provide accurate guidance in a specific situation, then a more specific rule should

a. Hasty generalizations. Hasty generalizations occur when someone draws conclusions from too few examples, or someone draws conclusions from an atypical example.

b. Accident. The informal fallacy of accident occurs when someone fails to recognize that an argument is based on an exception to a rule.

c. False cause. The fallacy of false cause occurs when someone confuses a temporal order of events with causality, or when someone oversimplifies a very complex causal network.

d. False analogy. False analogy occurs when someone uses an analogy for which key aspects of the two elements being compared do not match up.

e. Poisoning the well. Being committed to a position to such an extent that someone explains away everything that is offered in opposition to his or her position is referred to as "poisoning the well."

f. Begging the question (circularity). Begging the question involves making a claim and then arguing on its behalf by advancing grounds whose meaning is simply equivalent to that of the original claim.

g. Evading the issue. Evading the issue is "sidestepping" an issue by changing the topic.

h. Appealing to authority. Appealing to authority refers to invoking authority as the "last word" on an issue.

i. Arguing against the person. Rejecting a claim on the basis of derogatory facts (real or alleged) about the person making the claim is referred to as arguing against the person.

j. Arguing from ignorance. Arguing that a claim is justified simply because its opposite cannot be proved is called arguing from ignorance.

k. Appealing to the people. Appealing to the people is an attempt to justify a claim on the basis of its popularity.

l. Appealing to emotion. Using an emotion-laden or "sob story" as proof for a claim is referred to as appealing to emotion.

m. Appealing to force. Appealing to force is the use of threats as a way of establishing the validity of a claim.

n. Contradiction. The fallacy of contradiction occurs when information which is in direct opposition is presented within the same argument.

Figure 4.5. Informal Fallacies

be generated. *Unusualness rules* state that if a situation has an unexpected property relative to the rule that governs the situation, a conditioned element should be added to the original rule. The *rule of large numbers* states that when generating a rule based on a sample of events or elements, the rule should be generated under the assumption that it applies to all elements in the set; however, a strength parameter should be attached to the rule proportionate with the number of events or elements that have been sampled—the more events or elements, the stronger the rule. *Regulation rules* state that if an individual has a rule of the following form: "If you want to do *X*, then you must first do *Y*," then a rule like the following should be generated: "If you do not do *Y*, then you cannot do *X*" (p. 42).

Deduction is generally thought of as reasoning from the general to the specific. Deductive inferences are also rule-based. Holland et al. (1986) identify two categories of deductive rules: *synchronic* and *diachronic*. Synchronic rules are atemporal in nature and form the basis for classification and categorization. There are two types of synchronic rules: *categorical* and *associative*. These are exemplified as follows:

1. Categorical

   If an object is a dog, then it is an animal.

   If an object is a large, slender dog with very long white and gold hair, then it is a collie.

2. Associative

   If an object is a dog, then activate the "cat" concept.

   If an object is a dog, then activate the "bone" concept.

Diachronic rules deal with basic relationships of cause/effect and temporal order. There are two types of diachronic rules: *predictor* and *effector.* These are exemplified in the following:

1. Predictor

   If a person annoys a dog, then the dog will growl.

   If a person whistles to a dog, then the dog will come to the person.

2. Effector

   If a dog chases you, then run away.

   If a dog approaches you with a wagging tail, then pet it.

Even more specific rules have been proposed by some psychologists (see Braine, 1978) as the basis for deduction. These rules are sometimes referred to as a form of "mental logic." Johnson-Laird (1983; Johnson-Laird & Byrne, 1991) has developed a theory of deduction that relies on symbolic "tokens."

The process of generalizing, as defined in the New Taxonomy, is neither purely inductive nor purely deductive. In fact, it is probably safe to say that no mental process is purely inductive or purely deductive. Rather, scholars assert that reasoning is often more "messy" and nonlinear than earlier definitions suggest (Deely, 1982; Eco, 1976, 1979, 1984; Medawar, 1967; Percy, 1975). Many philosophers have advanced the concept of *retroduction* as a more fruitful approach to understanding the nature of inferential thinking. Retroduction is the act of generating and shaping an idea based on one or more cases. Sometimes inferences made during this process are more inductive in nature; sometimes they are more deductive in nature. Generalizing within the New Taxonomy, then, is best described as a retroductive process that is oriented more toward induction than deduction, but involves both during different aspects of the process. To illustrate, a student is involved in the analytic process of generalizing by constructing a new generalization about "regions" from three generalizations that have already been presented in class.

Marzano and others (Marzano et al., 1997) have identified a set of steps students might follow when generalizing:

1. Focus on specific pieces of information or observations. Try not to assume anything.

2. Look for patterns or connections in the information you have identified.

3. Make a general statement that explains the patterns or connections you have observed.

4. Make more observations to see if your generalization holds up; if it does not, change it as necessary.

Specifying

As defined in the New Taxonomy, specifying is the process of generating new applications of a known generalization or principle. As the previous discussion illustrates, there is probably no purely inductive versus deductive mental process. However, some tend to be more inductive or deductive in nature. Where the analytic process of generalizing is more inductive, the analytic process of specifying tends to be more deductive in nature. To illustrate, a student is involved in the analytic process of specifying by identifying a new situation or new phenomenon that is governed by Bernoulli's principle. The student has taken known principles and identified a new application previously not known to the individual. Marzano et al. (1997) have identified a process that might be followed during specification:

1. Identify the specific situation that is being considered or studied.

2. Identify the generalizations or principles that apply to the specific situation.

3. Make sure that the specific situation meets the conditions that have to be in place for those generalizations or principles to apply.

4. If the generalizations or principles do apply, identify what is known about the specific situation, that is, what conclusions can be drawn or what predictions can be made.

Relationship to Bloom's Taxonomy

The cognitive category of analysis in the New Taxonomy incorporates elements from at least three levels of Bloom's Taxonomy. Matching in the New Taxonomy appears to be similar to what Bloom refers to as analysis of relationships within level 4.0 (analysis) of his taxonomy. Classification in the New Taxonomy appears to be similar to what Bloom refers to as identifying a set of abstract relations within level 5.0 (synthesis). Error analysis in the New Taxonomy is similar to what is referred to as "judgments in terms of internal evidence" within level 6.0 (evaluation) of Bloom's Taxonomy. It is also similar to analysis of organizing principles within level 4.0 (analysis) of Bloom's Taxonomy. Generalizing and specifying in the New Taxonomy appear to be similar to or embedded in many components of levels 4, 5, and 6 of Bloom's Taxonomy. In short, analysis within the New Taxonomy incorporates a variety of aspects of the three highest levels of Bloom's Taxonomy.

Level 4: Knowledge Utilization (Cognitive System)

As their name implies, knowledge utilization processes are those that individuals employ when they wish to accomplish a specific task. For example, an engineer might use his or her knowledge of Bernoulli's principle to solve a specific problem related to lift in the design of a new type of aircraft. Specific tasks, then, are the venue in which knowledge is rendered useful to individuals.

In the New Taxonomy, four general categories of knowledge utilization tasks have been identified: (1) decision making, (2) problem solving, (3) experimental inquiry, and (4) investigation.

Decision Making

The process of decision making is used when an individual must select between two or more alternatives (Baron, 1982, 1985; Halpern, 1984). Metaphorically, decision making might be described as the process by which an individual answers questions like, What is the best way ____? or Which of these
is most suitable? For example, individuals are engaged in decision making
when they use their knowledge of specific locations within a city to identify
the best site for a new park.

There are a number of models describing the process of decision making,
including those by Wales, Nardi, and Stager (1986), Halpern (1984), and
Ehrenberg, Ehrenberg, and Durfee (1979). Steps and heuristics commonly associated with the overall process of decision making include

- Identification of alternatives

- Assignment of values to alternatives

- Determination of probability of success

- Determination of alternatives having highest value and highest probability of success (Baron, 1985; Wales, Nardi, & Stager, 1986; Wales &
  Stager, 1977)

Problem Solving

The process of problem solving is used when an individual attempts to accomplish a goal for which an obstacle exists (Rowe, 1985). Metaphorically,
problem solving might be described as the process one engages in to answer
questions such as, How will I overcome this obstacle? or How will I reach my
goal, but still meet these conditions? At its core, then, a defining characteristic
of a problem is an obstacle or limiting condition. For example, if a young
woman wishes to be at a specific location some miles from her home by a certain time and her car breaks down, she has a problem: She is attempting to accomplish a goal (i.e., to transport herself to a specific location) and an obstacle
has arisen (i.e., her usual mode of transportation is not available). To address
this problem effectively, she would have to use knowledge about different
methods of transportation that are alternatives to taking her car (e.g., taking
the bus, calling a friend) as well as options for fixing her car within the available time.

Steps and heuristics commonly associated with problem solving include

- Identification of obstacle to goal

- Possible re-analysis of goal

- Identification of alternatives
- Evaluation of alternatives
- Selection and execution of alternatives (Halpern, 1984; Rowe, 1985; Sternberg, 1987)

Experimental Inquiry

Experimental inquiry is the process of generating and testing hypotheses for the purpose of understanding some physical or psychological phenomenon. Metaphorically, experimental inquiry might be described as the process used when answering questions such as, How can this be explained? or Based on this explanation, what can be predicted? For example, a man is involved in experimental inquiry when he generates and tests a hypothesis about the effect a new airplane wing design will have on lift and drag.

The steps and heuristics commonly associated with experimental inquiry include

- Making predictions based on known or hypothesized principles
- Designing a way to test the predictions
- Evaluating the validity of the principles based on the outcome of the test (Halpern, 1984; Ross, 1988)

Investigation

Investigation is the process of generating and testing hypotheses about past, present, or future events. Metaphorically, investigation may be described as the process one goes through when attempting to answer such questions as, What are the defining features of____? or How did this happen? or Why did this happen? or What would have happened if____? To illustrate, a student is involved in investigation when he or she examines possible explanations for the existence of "crop circles."

To some extent, the knowledge utilization process of investigation is similar to the knowledge utilization process of experimental inquiry in that hypotheses are generated and tested. However, it differs from experimental inquiry in that it employs different "rules of evidence." Specifically, the rules of evidence for investigation adhere to the criteria for sound argumentation described in the discussion of error analysis. That is, the evidence used to support a claim within an investigation is a well-constructed argument. However, the rules of evidence for experimental inquiry adhere to the criteria for statistical hypotheses testing.

Marzano et al. (1997) have identified steps or heuristics associated with the process of investigation:

- Identifying what is known or agreed upon regarding the phenomenon under investigation
- Identifying areas of confusion or controversy regarding the phenomenon
- Providing an answer for the confusion or controversy
- Presenting a logical argument for the proposed answer

Relationship to Bloom's Taxonomy

The overall category of knowledge utilization in the New Taxonomy seems most closely related to synthesis (level 5.0) of Bloom's Taxonomy. Although Bloom's synthesis category does not address knowledge utilization per se, it does focus on the generation of new products and new ideas. By definition, the knowledge utilization processes of the New Taxonomy generate new products of some sort. For example, decision making generates a new awareness as to the superiority of one alternative over others; problem solving generates a new process for accomplishing a goal; and so on.

Level 5: Metacognition

The metacognitive system has been described by researchers and theorists as responsible for monitoring, evaluating, and regulating the functioning of all other types of thought (Brown, 1984; Flavell, 1978; Meichenbaum & Asarnow, 1979). Taken together, these functions are sometimes referred to as responsible for "executive control" (Brown, 1978, 1980; Flavell, 1979, 1987; Sternberg, 1984a, 1984b, 1986a, 1986b). Within the New Taxonomy, the metacognitive system has four functions: (1) goal specification, (2) process monitoring, (3) monitoring clarity, and (4) monitoring accuracy.

Goal Specification

One of the primary tasks of the metacognitive system is to establish clear goals. As we shall see in the next section, it is the self-system that determines an individual's decision whether or not to engage in an activity. However, once the decision is made to engage, it is the metacognitive system that establishes a goal relative to that activity. In terms of the New Taxonomy, the goal-setting function of the metacognitive system is responsible for establishing clear learning goals for specific types of knowledge. For example, it would be through the goal specification function of the metacognitive system that students would establish a specific goal or goals in terms of increasing their understanding or use of specific information presented in a mathematics class.

As part of the goal-specification process, an individual will usually identify what Hayes (1981) refers to as a clear "end state"—what the goal will look like when completed. This might also include the identification of "milestones" to be accomplished along the way. Finally, it is the job of the goal specification function of the metacognitive system to develop a plan for accomplishing a given learning goal. This might include the resources that will be necessary and even timelines in which milestones and the end state will be accomplished. It is this type of thinking that has been described as "strategic" in nature (Paris, Lipson & Wixson, 1983).

Process Monitoring

The process monitoring component of the metacognitive system is a relatively specialized function that monitors the effectiveness of an algorithm, tactic, or process as it is being used in a task. It applies to mental and physical procedural knowledge, but not to information. For example, the metacognitive system will monitor how well the mental procedure of reading a bar graph or the physical procedure of shooting a free throw is being carried out.

Monitoring Clarity and Accuracy

Monitoring clarity and monitoring accuracy belong to a set of functions that some researchers refer to as "dispositional" (see Amabile, 1983; Brown, 1978, 1980; Costa, 1984, 1991; Ennis, 1985, 1987a, 1987b, 1989; Flavell, 1976, 1977; R. Paul, 1990; R. W. Paul, 1984, 1986a; Perkins, 1984, 1985, 1986). The term *disposition* is used to indicate that monitoring clarity and monitoring accuracy are ways in which an individual is or is not disposed to approach knowledge. For example, individuals might or might not have a tendency to monitor whether they are clear about information that has been learned or are accurate about information that has been learned. It should be noted that the use of such dispositions is not automatic. Rather, individuals must consciously decide to approach a given task with an eye toward clarity and accuracy. Perhaps for this reason, this aspect of metacognition has been associated with high intelligence or "intelligent behavior" (Costa, 1991).

In summary, the metacognitive system is in charge of conscious operations relative to knowledge that include goal setting, process monitoring, and monitoring for clarity and accuracy. Salomon and Globerson (1987) refer to such thinking as being "mindful":

> The individual can be expected to withhold or inhibit the evocation of a first, salient response, to examine and elaborate situational cues and underlying meanings that are relevant to the task to be accomplished, to generate or define alternative strategies, to gather information necessary for the choices to be made, to examine outcomes, to draw new connections and construct new structures and abstractions made by reflective type processes. (Salomon and Globerson, 1987, p. 625)

Relationship to Bloom's Taxonomy

No obvious corollary in Bloom's Taxonomy can be found to the metacognitive level as described in the New Taxonomy.

Level 6: Self-System Thinking

The self-system consists of an interrelated system of attitudes, beliefs, and emotions. It is the interaction of these attitudes, beliefs, and emotions that determines both motivation and attention. Specifically, the self-system determines whether an individual will engage in or disengage in a given task; it also determines how much energy the individual will bring to the task. Once the self-system has determined what will be attended to, the functioning of all other elements of thought (i.e., the metacognitive system, the cognitive system, and the knowledge domains) are, to a certain extent, dedicated or determined. This is why the act of the self-system's selecting a task has been referred to as "crossing the Rubicon" (Garcia & Pintrich, 1993; Pintrich & Garcia, 1992).

There are four types of self-system thinking that are relevant to the New Taxonomy: (1) examining importance, (2) examining efficacy, (3) examining emotional response, and (4) examining overall motivation.

Examining Importance

One of the key determinants of whether an individual attends to a given type of knowledge is whether that individual considers the knowledge important. Obviously, if students consider the skill of reading a contour map important, they will be more likely to expend time and energy developing this mental skill.

What an individual considers to be important is probably a function of the extent to which it meets one of two conditions: it is perceived as instrumental in satisfying a basic need, or it is perceived as instrumental in the attainment of a personal goal. As explained by psychologists such as Maslow (1968), human beings have evolutionarily designed needs that might even exist in somewhat of a hierarchic structure, in which needs such as physical safety, food, and shelter are more basic than needs such as companionship and acceptance. If a specific knowledge component is perceived as being instrumental in meeting one or more of these needs, it will be considered important by an individual. For example, if a boy perceives that the ability to read a contour map will increase his chances of physical safety while participating in a camping trip, he will probably choose to put considerable time and energy into acquiring that mental skill.

Other than the extent to which it helps one meet basic needs, a knowledge component can be perceived as important because it is seen to be instrumental in attaining some personal goal. For example, if a young man perceives that reading a contour map will help him attain a lifelong goal of becoming a forest ranger, he will probably choose to put time and energy into acquiring this skill.

The exact source of these personal goals is, to date, a bit of a mystery. Some would assert that personal goals are functions of one's environment: Our need for acceptance propels us to construct personal goals that will increase our sense of esteem within our culture (see Bandura, 1977, 1982, 1991, 1993, 1996, 1997). Others would assert that personal goals are an outgrowth of more deeply held beliefs regarding the purpose of life. For example, philosophers such as Frankl (1967) and Buber (1958) have demonstrated that beliefs about one's ultimate purpose are a central feature of one's psychological makeup. A strong case can be made that this set of beliefs ultimately exerts control over all other elements in the self-system. To illustrate, assume that a young woman believes that her purpose in life (or one of her purposes) is to use her talents to contribute to the benefit of others. As a consequence, she will consider those things important that contribute to this goal. She will then encode specific persons, situations, events, and the like as important or not, based on whether they are perceived as instrumental in realizing this purpose.

Regardless of their explanations regarding the ultimate source of personal goals, most psychologists agree that they are a primary factor in one's perception of what is important.

Examining Efficacy

Bandura's (1977, 1982, 1991, 1993, 1996, 1997) theories and research have brought the role of beliefs about efficacy to the attention of psychologists and educators alike. In simple terms, beliefs about efficacy address the extent to which individuals believe they have the resources, ability, or power to change a situation. Relative to the New Taxonomy, examining efficacy would involve examining the extent to which individuals believe they have the ability, power, or necessary resources to gain competence relative to a specific knowledge component. If Carla believes she does not have the requisite ability, power, or resources to gain competence in a specific skill, this might greatly lessen her motivation to learn that knowledge even though she perceives it as important.

Bandura's research indicates that a sense of efficacy is not necessarily a generalizable construct. Rather, an individual might have a strong sense of efficacy in one situation, yet feel relatively powerless in another. Seligman's research (1990, 1994) also attests to the situational nature of one's sense of efficacy and underscores the importance of these beliefs. He has found that a low sense of efficacy can result in a pattern of behavior that he refers to as "learned helplessness."

Examining Emotional Response

The influence of emotion in human motivation is becoming increasingly clear. Given the biology of emotions, many brain researchers assert that these emotions are involved in almost every aspect of human behavior. Specifically, a good case can be made for the contention that emotion exerts a controlling influence over human thought. This case is well articulated in LeDoux's *The Emotional Brain: The Mysterious Underpinnings of Emotional Life* (1996).

Among other things, as a result of his analysis of the research on emotions, LeDoux concludes that human beings (a) have little direct control over their emotional reactions, and (b) once emotions occur, they become powerful motivators of future behavior. Relative to humans' lack of control over emotions, LeDoux notes:

> Anyone who has tried to fake an emotion, or who has been the recipient of a faked one, knows all too well the futility of the attempt. While conscious control over emotions is weak, emotions can flood consciousness. This is so because the wiring of the brain at this point in our evolutionary history is such that connections from the emotional systems to the cognitive systems are stronger than connections from the cognitive systems to the emotional systems. (p. 19)

Relative to the power of emotions once they occur, LeDoux explains:

> They chart the course of moment-to-moment action as well as set the sails toward long-term achievements. But our emotions can also get us into trouble. When fear becomes anxiety, desire gives way to greed, or annoyance turns to anger, anger to hatred, friendship to envy, love to obsession, or pleasure to addiction, our emotions start working

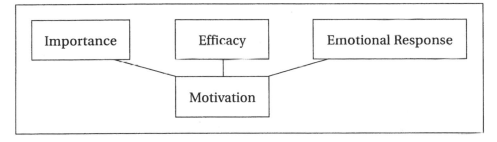

Figure 4.6. Aspects of Motivation

against us. Mental health is maintained by emotional hygiene, and mental problems, to a large extent, reflect a breakdown of emotional order. Emotions can have both useful and pathological conse quences. (pp. 19-20)

For LeDoux, then, emotions are primary motivators that often outstrip an individual's system of values and beliefs relative to their influence on human behavior.

Relative to the New Taxonomy, examining emotions involves analyzing the extent to which an individual has an emotional response to a given knowledge component and the part that response plays in one's motivation.

Examining Overall Motivation

As might be inferred from the previous discussion, an individual's motivation to initially learn or increase competence in a given knowledge component is a function of three factors: (1) perceptions of its importance, (2) perceptions of efficacy relative to learning or increasing competency in the knowledge component, and (3) one's emotional response to the knowledge component. This is depicted in Figure 4.6.

Given this set of relationships, one can operationally describe different levels of motivation. Specifically, high motivation to learn or increase competence relative to a given knowledge component will exist under the following conditions:

1. The individual perceives the knowledge component as important, and

2. The individual believes that he or she has the necessary ability, power, or resources to learn or increase his or her competence relative to the knowledge component, and/or

3. The individual has a positive emotional response to the knowledge component

Low motivation occurs under the following conditions:

1. The individual perceives the knowledge component to be unimportant, and/or

2. The individual believes that he or she does not have the necessary ability, power, or resources to learn or increase his or her competence relative to the knowledge component, and/or

3. The individual has a negative emotional response to the knowledge component

It is important to note that these three self-system determiners of motivation are probably not equal in terms of their effect on motivation. In fact, it is likely that a perception of importance can override a perceived lack of efficacy and a negative emotional response. For example, a mother will be highly motivated to stop an oncoming car that is about to strike her young child. The mother surely does not believe that she has the physical power to stop the car (i.e., she has a low perception of efficacy in this situation) and she surely would have negative emotion associated with being struck by the car herself. However, her child's safety is such an important goal to her that it overrides or outweighs the other two elements.

In terms of the New Taxonomy, examining motivation is the process of identifying one's level of motivation to learn or increase competence in a given knowledge component and then identifying the interrelationships between one's beliefs about importance, beliefs about efficacy, and emotional response that govern one's level of motivation.

Relationship to Bloom's Taxonomy

As in the case with metacognition, the self-system component of the New Taxonomy has no obvious corollary in Bloom's Taxonomy.

Revisiting the Hierarchical Nature of the New Taxonomy

The fact that the New Taxonomy has a fairly strong hierarchical structure in terms of the three systems of thought—self-, metacognitive, and cognitive— has already been discussed in Chapter 2. That hierarchical structure is based on flow of processing. To review briefly, the self-system is the first line of processing: It determines the extent to which a student will be motivated to learn a given knowledge component. Given that the self-system has determined

Conscious	Level 6:	Self-System Processes
	Level 5:	Metacognitive Processes
	Level 4:	Knowledge Utilization Processes
	Level 3:	Analysis Processes
	Level 2:	Comprehension Processes
Automatic	Level 1:	Retrieval Processes

Figure 4.7. Conscious Control and the Levels of the New Taxonomy

that knowledge is important enough to learn, the next system to be engaged is the metacognitive system. Its task is to establish clear learning goals relative to the knowledge, then plan for and carry out those goals in as precise a manner as possible. Under the direction of the metacognitive system, the elements of the cognitive system are then employed. As we have seen, the cognitive system is responsible for processes as simple as retrieval and as complex as using the knowledge in a new context.

The three systems within the New Taxonomy are also hierarchical relative to the level of consciousness required to control their execution. Whereas cognitive processes require a certain degree of awareness and conscious thought to be executed in a controlled fashion, the metacognitive processes probably require more. That is, learning goals cannot be set, nor can accuracy be monitored, for example, without a fair degree of mental energy. Finally, examining self-system processes such as importance and emotional response probably represents a level of introspection and conscious thought not normally engaged in.

Consciousness of processing, necessary for control, is a characteristic that also discloses the hierarchic nature of the cognitive system, which consists of the first four levels of the New Taxonomy—retrieval, comprehension, analysis, and knowledge utilization. The retrieval processes, as described in the New Taxonomy, can be executed automatically; the comprehension processes require slightly more conscious thought, and analysis processes still more. Finally, the utilization processes require even more conscious processing.

Given that the metacognitive processes require more conscious thought than the cognitive processes and the self-system processes require more conscious thought than the metacognitive processes, a taxonomy of six levels can be established. This is depicted in Figure 4.7.

This said, it is important to realize that the six levels of the New Taxonomy do not represent levels of complexity. The processes within the self-system are not more complex than the processes within the metacognitive system, and so on. This is in contrast to Bloom's Taxonomy, which attempts to use processing difficulty as the critical feature separating one level from the next. In addition, it is important to note that the New Taxonomy makes no claims that the components within the self- and metacognitive systems are themselves hierarchical in nature. For example, there is no necessary ordering of the processes of examining importance, examining efficacy, and examining emotional response in terms of levels of consciousness.

Taxonomy of Objectives

The six levels of the New Taxonomy make for a rather straightforward taxonomy of objectives for any type of knowledge. The objectives or expectations within each level require more conscious processing on the part of students than is required at lower levels. Figure 4.8 presents an articulation of objectives at all six levels of the New Taxonomy.

These six levels of processing interact with the three knowledge domains described in Chapter 3. The next chapter details the specifics of these interactions.

Summary

This chapter has described the six levels of the New Taxonomy within the context of three systems of thought—cognitive, metacognitive, and self-system. The cognitive system includes processes that address retrieval, comprehension, analysis, and knowledge utilization. The metacognitive system includes processes that address goal specification, process monitoring, and disposition monitoring. The self-system includes processing dedicated to examining importance, examining efficacy, and examining emotional response. It is the interaction of these elements that dictate one's motivation and attention.

Level 6: Self

Examining Importance	The student can identify how important the knowledge is to him or her and the reasoning underlying this perception.
Examining Efficacy	The student can identify beliefs about his or her ability to improve competence or understanding relative to knowledge and the reasoning underlying this perception.
Examining Emotional Response	The student can identify emotional responses to knowledge and the reasons for these responses.
Examining Motivation	The student can identify his or her level of motivation to improve competence or understanding relative to knowledge and the reasons for this level of motivation.

Level 5: Metacognition

Goal Specification	The student can set a plan for goals relative to the knowledge.
Process Monitoring	The student can monitor the execution of the knowledge.
Monitoring Clarity	The student can determine the extent to which he or she has clarity about the knowledge.
Monitoring Accuracy	The student can determine the extent to which he or she is accurate about the knowledge.

Level 4: Utilization

Decision Making	The student can use the knowledge to make decisions or can make decisions about the use of knowledge.
Problem Solving	The student can use the knowledge to solve problems or can solve problems about the knowledge.
Experimental Inquiry	The student can use the knowledge to generate and test hypotheses or can generate and test hypotheses about the knowledge.
Investigation	The student can use the knowledge to conduct investigations or can conduct investigations about the knowledge.

Figure 4.8. Objectives for the Levels of the New Taxonomy

Level 3: Analysis

Matching	The student can identify important similarities and differences between knowledge.
Classifying	The student can identify superordinate and subordinate categories related to knowledge.
Error Analysis	The student can identify errors in the presentation or use of knowledge.
Generalizing	The student can construct new generalizations or principles based on knowledge.
Specifying	The student can identify specific applications or logical consequences of knowledge.

Level 2: Comprehension

Synthesis	The student can identify the basic structure of knowledge and the critical as opposed to noncritical characteristics.
Representation	The student can identify or recognize features of information but does not necessarily understand the structure of knowledge or can differentiate critical from noncritical components.

Level 1: Retrieval

Recall	The student can identify or recognize features of information but does not necessarily understand the structure of knowledge or can differentiate critical from noncritical components.
Execution	The student can perform a procedure without significant error but does not necessarily understand how and why the procedure works.

Figure 4.8. Continued

CHAPTER 5

The New Taxonomy and the Three Knowledge Domains

As described in Chapter 3, knowledge within any subject area can be organized into the domains of information, mental processes, and psycho motor processes. The six levels of the New Taxonomy interact differently with these three knowledge domains. In this chapter, we discuss each of the three knowledge domains in light of the six levels of the New Taxonomy. Before doing so, however, it is worth underscoring the difference between this approach and that taken in Bloom's Taxonomy.

Bloom's Taxonomy addressed the differences in types of knowledge at the first level only. There, Bloom distinguished between terms versus details versus generalizations, and so on. However, these distinctions were not carried through to the other five levels of the taxonomy. That is, no discussion was provided as to how Bloom's process of evaluation, for instance, is different for details than it is for generalizations.

In contrast, as articulated in this chapter, the New Taxonomy explicitly defines the manner in which each of its six levels interacts with the three knowledge domains. In effect, then, the New Taxonomy is two-dimensional in nature: One dimension is the six levels of the taxonomy, the other is the three knowledge domains. This is depicted in Figure 5.1.

Level 1: Knowledge Retrieval

Retrieval involves the simple recall or execution of knowledge. Whether knowledge is recalled versus executed is a function of the exact type of knowledge involved. As described in Chapters 3 and 4, the information domain involves declarative knowledge only. Declarative knowledge can be recalled but not executed. The domains of mental and psychomotor procedures involve procedural knowledge. Knowledge in these two domains can be both recalled and executed.

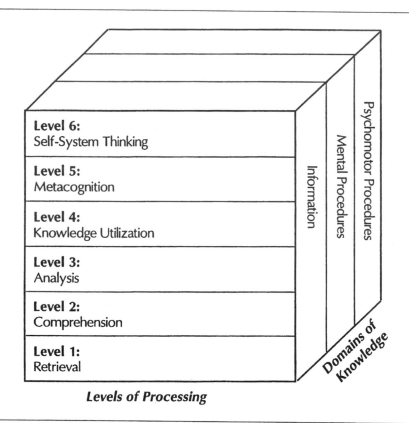

Figure 5.1. Two-Dimensional Model

Objectives that relate to retrieval across the three knowledge domains are presented in Figure 5.2.

Retrieval deals with the transfer of knowledge from permanent memory to working memory. There is no expectation that the student will know the knowledge in depth, will be able to identify the basic structure of the knowledge (or its critical versus noncritical elements), or will use it to accomplish complex goals. These are all expectations for higher levels of the New Taxonomy.

For students to demonstrate recall of simple details within the domain of information, they must produce or recognize accurate, but not necessarily critical, information about a vocabulary term, fact, time sequence, cause/ effect sequence, or episode. A question that would elicit recall about a specific vocabulary term is:

We have been studying the term synapse. Briefly describe what it means.

A question that would elicit recall of a specific cause/effect sequence is:

Jean Valjean was first sentenced to the galleys for which of the following:

Information			
Details	Recall		When asked about a specific detail, the student can produce or recognize related information.
	Execution		
Organizing Ideas	Recall		When presented with a principle or generalization, the individual can produce or recognize related information.
	Execution		

Mental Procedures			
Skills	Recall		When asked, the student can describe the general nature and purpose of the mental skill.
	Execution		When prompted, the student can perform the mental skill without significant error.
Processes	Recall		When asked, the student can describe the general nature and purpose of the mental process.
	Execution		When prompted, the student can perform the process without significant error.

Psychomotor Procedures			
Skills	Recall		When asked, the student can describe the general nature and purpose of the psychomotor skill.
	Execution		When prompted, the student can perform the psychomotor skill without significant error.
Processes	Recall		When asked, the student can describe the general nature and purpose of the psychomotor process.
	Execution		When prompted, the student can perform the psychomotor process without significant error.

Figure 5.2. Retrieval Objectives

1. Stealing a loaf of bread
2. Stealing the Bishop's candlesticks
3. Not paying taxes on a cow he bought
4. Refusing to join the French army

Demonstrating knowledge recall for organizing ideas within the domain of information involves articulating or recognizing examples of a generalization or a principle. For example, a student demonstrates recall of an organizing idea by producing examples of generalizations about the origin of life. A question that would elicit this type of thinking is:

We have been studying examples of the generalization that "all life comes from life and produces its own kind of living organism." Identify two examples of this that we have studied.

A question that would elicit knowledge recall relative to a principle is:

Coulomb's law of electrostatic attraction states that "the force of attraction or repulsion between two charged bodies is directly proportional to the product of the charges, and inversely proportional to the square of the distance between them." Describe two consequences we have studied about this law.

It is important to note that both questions above make mention of the fact that examples or applications have already been addressed (i.e., Identify two examples . . . we have studied). This is so because recall, by definition, involves information that is known, not information newly generated. Asking students to generate new examples of a generalization or principle is better described as analysis (Level 3 of the New Taxonomy) as opposed to simple retrieval.

In terms of the domain of mental procedures, knowledge retrieval involves both recall and execution. Knowledge recall relative to a mental skill would involve retrieval of information about the basic purpose of the skill and/or situations in which it is used. For example, a student would be demonstrating knowledge recall relative to the mental skill of reading a contour map by articulating or recognizing common uses of the skill. A question that would elicit this type of thinking is:

What are some situations in which a contour map is useful?

As described previously, recall does not necessarily imply the ability to actually perform a procedure. Performance is demonstrated when a student executes the procedure. For example, a student demonstrates execution of the skill of reading a contour map by actually reading and interpreting such a map. A question that would engage the student in knowledge execution is:

You have been given a contour map of the area surrounding our school. Describe some of the information it provides about this area.

As is the case with skills, retrieval of mental processes involves both recall and execution. For example, a student demonstrates recall of the mental process of using a specific type of word-processing software (e.g., WordPerfect) by citing or recognizing situations in which the process is useful. A question that would elicit this type of thinking is:

Identify situations for which the word-processing program, Word-Perfect, is highly useful.

A student demonstrates knowledge execution by actually performing the process. A task that would elicit this type of thinking is:

On your desk you will find a copy of a letter. Using the program, Word-Perfect, type this letter, save it, and print it out on letterhead paper.

In terms of knowledge retrieval, psychomotor skills and processes follow the same patterns as do mental skills and processes. Questions and commands that would elicit recall and execution of the psychomotor skill of stretching the hamstring muscles are:

Recall:

We have been examining the proper technique for stretching the hamstrings. What are situations in which it is useful to use this technique?

Execution:

Demonstrate the proper method of stretching the hamstring muscles.

Questions and commands that would elicit recall and execution of the psychomotor process of warming up prior to vigorous exercise are:

Recall:

Describe why it is important to warm up before strenuous exercise.

Execution:

Demonstrate a warm-up routine that would be effective prior to any type of vigorous physical activity.

Level 2: Comprehension

The comprehension processes require more of students than do the knowledge retrieval processes. Where knowledge retrieval involves recall or execution of knowledge as learned, comprehension involves the identification and
representation of the more important versus less important aspects of that
knowledge. There are two related comprehension processes: synthesis and
representation.

Synthesis

Synthesis involves reducing knowledge down to its key parts. As described in
Chapter 4, in technical terms, synthesis involves creating a macrostructure for
knowledge—a parsimonious accounting of the key elements of the knowledge
usually at a more general level than originally experienced. Figure 5.3 lists objectives for knowledge synthesis across the three knowledge domains.

In some situations, synthesis can be applied to details. Since synthesis, by
definition, involves identifying essential versus nonessential elements, a detail must have a fairly complex structure to be amenable to synthesis. For example, the events occurring at the Alamo might be complex enough to war-
rant the comprehension process of synthesis. At the level of recall, students
would be expected to remember the general nature of these events only. At the
level of synthesis, however, students would be expected to identify those
events that were critical to the final outcome versus those that were not. A
question that would elicit knowledge synthesis relative to this event is:

> Identify those events that happened at the Alamo that were critical to
> its outcome versus those that were not.

Given their nature—specifically their inherent complexity—organizing
ideas of all types are highly amenable to synthesis. However, the process of
synthesis is somewhat different for principles than it is for generalizations.
Relative to principles, the process of synthesis results in an understanding of
relationships between the variables that are addressed in the principle. As described in Chapter 3, relationships between variables can take many forms.
For example, the increase in one variable is associated with an increase in the
other, or an increase in one variable is associated with a decrease in the other.
To demonstrate synthesis of a principle, then, a student must describe the
variables associated with the principle and the precise nature of their relationship. For example, a student would demonstrate synthesis of a principle
by identifying and describing the relationship between the number of lemmings in an Arctic habitat and the number of caribou in the same habitat, or
by describing the relationship between the amount of carbonate dissolved in

Information	
Details	The student can identify the essential versus nonessential elements of a specific detail.
Organizing Ideas	The student can identify the defining characteristics of a generalization or a principle.
Mental Procedures	
Skills	The student can describe the steps involved in a mental skill.
Processes	The student can describe the major aspects of a mental process.
Psychomotor Procedures	
Skills	The student can identify the steps involved in a psychomotor skill.
Processes	The student can identify the major aspects of a psychomotor process.

Figure 5.3. Synthesis Objectives

the water of a river and the number of clams in that river. The following questions would elicit the process of synthesis as they relate to these examples:

1. There is a relationship between the number of lemmings in the Arctic habitat and the number of caribou in the same habitat. Describe that relationship. Be careful to include all the major factors that affect this relationship.

2. Describe the relationship between the number of clams in a river and the amount of carbonate dissolved in the water. What are some of the factors affecting this relationship, and how do they affect it?

Synthesis as it relates to generalization involves the identification of critical versus noncritical attributes of the generalization. Recall from Chapter 3 that a generalization is a statement about a class of persons, places, things, events, or abstractions. Synthesis as it relates to generalizations, then, involves identifying the defining characteristics of a class as opposed to related, but not defining, characteristics. For example, a student would demonstrate synthesis of a generalization about golden retrievers by identifying characteristics that define this class of canine as opposed to those that are associated with the category but do not define it. A question that would elicit this type of synthesis is:

What are the defining features of golden retrievers versus those features that are associated with this type of dog but are not defining
characteristics?

Synthesis of a mental skill or process involves identifying and articulating
the various steps of that skill or process as well as the order of those steps. A
question that would elicit synthesis of the mental skill of reading a bar graph is:

Describe the steps you go through when you read a bar graph. Explain
whether those steps must be performed in any specific order.

A question that would elicit synthesis relative to the mental process of
using WordPerfect is:

Describe the steps you must go through to write a letter, save it, and
print it out using WordPerfect. How do the various parts of this process relate to one another?

Synthesis applies to psychomotor skills and processes in the same way it
applies to mental skills and processes. A student demonstrates synthesis relative to the psychomotor skill of making a backhand shot in tennis by describing the component parts of the action. A student demonstrates synthesis relative to the process of returning a serve in tennis by describing the skills and
strategies involved and their interactions. Questions that would elicit this type
of thinking are:

1. Describe the best way to make a backhand shot. What are the crit-
    ical elements in hitting a good backhand?
2. Explain the skills and strategies involved in returning a serve. How
    do these skills and strategies interact with one another?

Representation

The comprehension process of representation involves depicting knowledge
in some type of nonlinguistic or symbolic form. Figure 5.4 lists objectives for
the comprehension process of representation across the three knowledge domains.

It is important to note that each of the descriptions in Figure 5.4 empha-
sizes the need for accuracy in the student's representation. Indeed, as described in Chapter 4, the process of representation assumes an accurate synthesis of knowledge. That is, representation, by definition, is an encoding or
translation of the product of an effective synthesis of knowledge. Conse-

Information		
	Details	The student can accurately represent the major aspects of a detail in nonlinguistic or symbolic form.
	Organizing Ideas	The student can accurately represent the major components of a generalization or principle and their relationship in nonlinguistic or symbolic form.
Mental Procedures		
	Skills	The student can accurately represent the component parts of a mental skill in nonlinguistic or symbolic form.
	Processes	The student can accurately represent the component parts of a mental process in nonlinguistic or symbolic form.
Psychomotor Procedures		
	Skills	The student can accurately represent the component parts of a psychomotor skill in nonlinguistic or symbolic form.
	Processes	The student can accurately represent the component parts of a psychomotor process in nonlinguistic or symbolic form.

Figure 5.4. Representation Objectives

quently, to demonstrate representation of knowledge, a student would necessarily have synthesized that knowledge.

Representation of details can be elicited from students by fairly straightforward requests. For example, if a teacher wished to determine students' ability to represent their understanding of the term *heredity*, he or she might ask a question like the following:

In this unit we have used the term *heredity*. Illustrate what you consider to be the important aspect of the term using a graphic representation or a pictograph.

If a teacher wished to elicit the process of representation about a specific event, he or she might make the following request of students:

Represent the key events that occurred when Iraq invaded Kuwait in 1989.

Representation of details can be done in a wide variety of ways. For example, one student might choose to represent the key information about heredity as a graphic organizer, while another might choose to represent it as a pictograph, and still another as a picture.

The appropriate forms of representation are somewhat more limited for organizing ideas. Specifically, as described in Chapter 4, generalizations lend themselves to certain types of representations and not others. One of the most common is that depicted in Figure 5.5 for a representation of the generalization that "dictators rise to power when countries are weak by promising them strength."

A question that would elicit representation relative to this generalization is:

> Design a graph that represents the generalization that "dictators rise to power when countries are weak by promising them strength."

Given that principles describe relationships between variables, they are commonly represented by graphs. For example, Figure 5.6 contains a graphic representation a student might construct to represent the relationship between the number of lemmings in an Arctic habitat and the number of caribou in the same habitat.

A question that would elicit this type of thinking is:

> Create a graph that represents the relationship between the number of lemmings in an Arctic habitat and the number of caribou in the same habitat.

Relative to both mental and psychomotor procedures, representation commonly involves the construction of a diagram or flow chart that depicts the flow of activity. For example, Figure 5.7 contains a diagrammatic representation a student might generate for the skill of reading a bar graph.

Questions that would elicit representation as it relates to mental and psychomotor procedures are:

> Mental skill: Draw a diagram that represents the thinking you go through when you read a bar graph.

> Mental process: Construct a diagram that represents that process of writing, storing, and printing a letter using WordPerfect.

> Psychomotor skill: Draw a diagram that represents the action involved in making a backhand stroke in tennis.

> Psychomotor process: Draw a diagram that represents what you do when you return a serve in tennis.

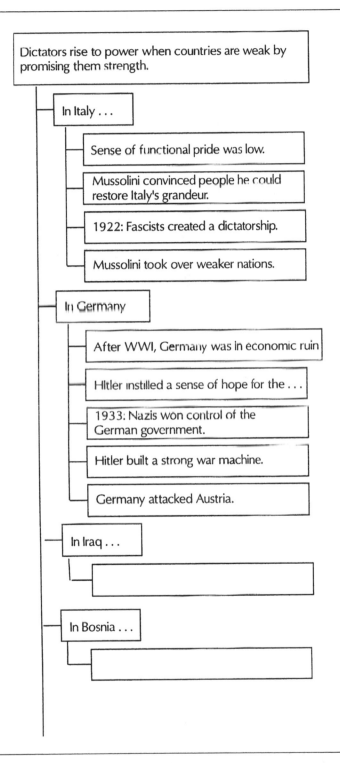

Figure 5.5. Representation for Generalization

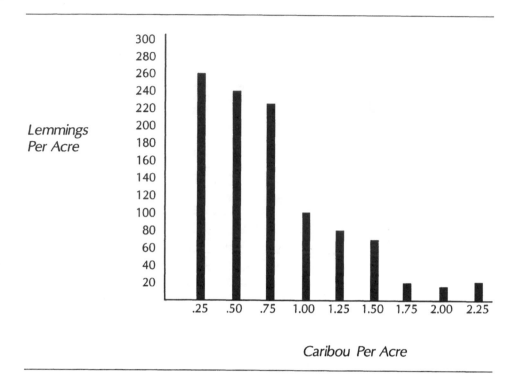

Figure 5.6. Representation for Principle

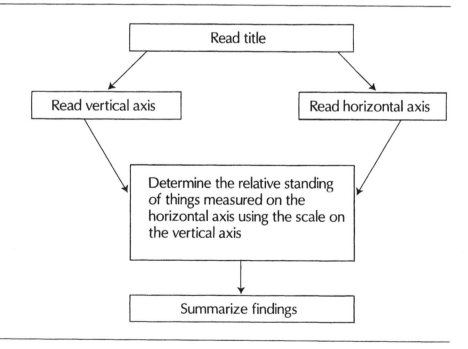

Figure 5.7. Representation for Skill

Level 3: Analysis

As described in Chapter 3, the analysis processes all involve examining knowledge in fine detail and, as a result, generating new conclusions. There are five analysis processes: (1) matching, (2) classification, (3) error analysis, (4) generalizing, and (5) specifying.

Matching

Matching involves identifying similarities and differences. Figure 5.8 lists matching objectives across the three knowledge domains.

As it relates to details, matching involves identifying the manner in which a term, fact, time sequence, cause/effect sequence, or episode is similar to, yet different from, similar structures. For example, Mary demonstrates her ability to match her knowledge of the events of the Battle of Gettysburg when she determines how it is similar to and different from other battles. A question that would elicit this type of thinking is:

Identify how the Battle of Gettysburg is similar to and different from the Battle of Atlanta.

Matching can involve more than two examples of a specific type of knowledge. For example, a student demonstrates the ability to match by organizing individuals from history into two or more groups based on their similarities. The following question would elicit this type of matching:

We have been studying a number of individuals who were important historically for one reason or another. Organize these individuals into two or more groups and explain how the individuals within each group are similar. Also explain how the individuals are different from group to group:

Alexander Graham Bell

Galileo

George Washington Carver

Louis Pasteur

Amelia Earhart

Sally Ride

John Glenn

Henry Ford

Eric the Red

Information	
Details	The student can identify how specific details are similar and different.
Organizing Ideas	The student can identify how a generalization or a principle is similar to and different from other generalizations and principles.
Mental Procedures	
Skills	The student can identify how mental skills are similar and different.
Processes	The student can identify how mental processes are similar and different.
Psychomotor Procedures	
Skills	The student can identify how psychomotor skills are similar and different.
Processes	The student can identify how psychomotor processes are similar and different.

Figure 5.8. Matching Objectives

> Ferdinand Magellan
>
> Jacques Cartier
>
> Martin Luther King, Jr.

Relative to organizing ideas, matching involves identifying how one principle or generalization is similar to and different from other principles or generalizations. A question that would elicit the process of matching relative to two principles is:

Below are two sets of variables found in nature. Identify the principle underlying each and explain how these principles are similar and different:

Set 1:

a. The amount of vegetation per square yard of soil

b. The amount of available nitrate salts in the same area of soil

Set 2:

a. Crop yield per acre of farmland cultivated in Illinois

b. Amount of soil nutrients per acre of farmland

Given the structure of principles, the main emphasis in matching them is on describing the similarities and differences between the relationships of the variables addressed in the principles. Generalizations, however, involve statements about classes of persons, places, living and nonliving things, events, and abstractions. Consequently, the process of matching generalizations is one of determining how the defining characteristics of two or more categories are similar and different. A question which would elicit this type of thinking is:

> We have been studying various characteristics of democratic politicians versus republican politicians. Identify how they are similar and different in specific characteristics.

Matching, as it relates to mental skills, involves identifying how two or more skills are similar and different in terms of the steps they involve. For example, a student would demonstrate the process of matching by articulating how reading a political map is similar to and different from reading a contour map. A question that would elicit this type of thinking is:

> Describe how reading a political map is similar to and different from reading a contour map.

Similarly, matching as it relates to mental processes involves identifying similarities and differences between the components of two or more processes. For example, a student demonstrates matching relative to the process of painting a picture using water colors by describing how this process is similar to and different from that of painting a picture using oils. A question that would elicit this type of thinking in students would be:

> Describe how the process of painting a picture using water colors is similar to and different from that of painting the same picture using oils.

Finally, matching, as it relates to psychomotor skills and processes, is identical to matching as it relates to mental skills and procedures. Examples of questions that would elicit matching relative to psychomotor procedures are:

> Psychomotor Skills: Describe how the process of hitting a backhand shot in tennis is similar to and different from the process of hitting a forehand shot.

> Psychomotor Processes: Describe how the process of returning a serve is similar to and different from the process of charging the net in tennis.

Classification

Classification as defined in the New Taxonomy goes beyond organizing items into groups or categories. That is a function of matching. Rather, classification involves identifying the superordinate categories knowledge belongs to as well as subordinate categories into which the knowledge can be organized. Figure 5.9 lists objectives for classification across the three knowledge domains.

In terms of details, classification involves the identification of superordinate categories only. For example, a student demonstrates the ability to classify a detail by identifying a general class or category of events to which the Battle of Gettysburg might belong. A question that would elicit this type of thinking is:

> To what general category of events would you assign the Battle of Gettysburg? Explain why you think this event falls into this category.

Since details by definition are quite specific, it is unlikely that they could be organized into subordinate classes or categories.

Classification of organizing ideas involves identifying superordinate categories as well as subordinate categories that are associated with a generalization or principle. To illustrate, a student would demonstrate classification of Bernoulli's principle by identifying a more general category of principles or theory to which it belongs. A question that would elicit this type of thinking is:

> We have been studying Bernoulli's principle. Identify a class of principles or a general theory to which it belongs. Explain the features of Bernoulli's principle that make it a member of the category you have identified.

A question that would elicit the identification of categories subordinate to Bernoulli's principle would be:

> Bernoulli's principle has many applications. Describe two or more categories of these applications.

In terms of mental skills, classification involves identifying superordinate categories only. Like details, skills are generally too specific to involve subordinate categories. For example, a student demonstrates classification of the skill of reading a bar graph by identifying a more general category of skill to which it belongs. Questions that would elicit this type of thinking are:

> To what category of skill does reading a bar graph belong? Explain why.
>
> What are the characteristics of reading a bar graph that make you say it belongs to this category?

Information	
Details	The student can identify the general category to which a specific detail belongs.
Organizing Ideas	The student can identify superordinate and subordinate categories for a generalization or principle.
Mental Procedures	
Skills	The student can identify superordinate categories for a mental skill.
Processes	The student can identify superordinate and subordinate categories for a mental process.
Psychomotor Procedures	
Skills	The student can identify superordinate categories for a psychomotor skill.
Processes	The student can identify superordinate and subordinate categories for a psychomotor process.

Figure 5.9. Classification Objectives

Classification of mental processes can involve the identification of superordinate and subordinate categories. Questions that would elicit this type of thinking are:

To what general category of processes does writing belong? What are the characteristics of writing that make it belong to this category?

Identify some types of writing that require slight differences in the steps you would use. How are these types of writing similar to, yet different from, each other?

Classification of psychomotor skills is similar to classification of mental skills. A question that would elicit classification of the psychomotor skill of stretching the hamstring muscles is:

We have been studying how to properly stretch the hamstring muscles. To what general category of activity does this skill belong? Explain what there is about stretching the hamstrings that justifies you assigning it to this category.

Classification of psychomotor processes is analogous to classification of mental processes. Questions that would elicit classification of the psychomotor process of warming up are:

> To what general category of processes does warming up belong? Explain why it belongs to this category.

> What are some specific types of warming up? Explain how these types are similar and different.

Error Analysis

Error analysis involves identifying logical errors in knowledge or processing errors in the execution of knowledge. As depicted in Figure 5.10, the analytical skill of error analysis plays out somewhat differently across the different knowledge domains. However, one characteristic common to all applications of error analysis is that they involve information that is false or inaccurate.

In terms of details, error analysis involves determining the extent to which new information is reasonable, given what the student already knows about the topic. For example, Alice demonstrates error analysis when she determines the plausibility of new information she is reading about the Battle of the Little Big Horn, based on what she already knows about that incident. A question that would elicit error analysis in this situation is:

> The attached article contains information about the Battle of the Little Big Horn that we have not addressed in class. Explain which information seems reasonable and why, and which information does not seem reasonable and why.

Error analysis, relative to organizing ideas, involves determining whether the new examples of a generalization or applications of a principle are logical. For example, a student demonstrates error analysis relative to known principles about the sun and its relationship to earth by identifying false conclusions someone might infer and explains why they are false. A question that would elicit this type of thinking is:

> John knows that you are most likely to get a sunburn if you are out in the sun between 11:00 a.m. and 1:00 p.m. He asks six of his friends why this is so. They each give him a different answer. Identify which of the answers are wrong and explain the errors made in each case:
>
> > Answer #1:　We are slightly closer to the sun at noon than in the morning or afternoon.

Information		
	Details	The student can determine the reasonableness of newly presented information regarding specific details.
	Organizing Ideas	The student can determine the reasonableness of new examples of a generalization or new applications of a principle.
Mental Procedures		
	Skills	The student can identify errors made during the execution of a mental skill.
	Processes	The student can identify errors made during the execution of a mental process.
Psychomotor Procedures		
	Skills	The student can identify errors made during the execution of a psychomotor skill.
	Processes	The student can identify errors made during the execution of a psychomotor process.

Figure 5.10. Error Analysis Objectives

Answer #2: More "burn" will be produced by the noon sun than by the morning or afternoon sun.

Answer #3: When the sun's rays fall straight down (directly) on a surface, more energy is received than when they fall indirectly on the surface.

Answer #4: When the sun is directly overhead, its rays pass through less atmosphere than when it is lower in the sky.

Answer #5: The air is usually warmer at noon than at any other time of the day.

Answer #6: The ultraviolet rays of sunlight are mainly responsible for sunburn.

In terms of mental skills and processes, error analysis involves identifying errors that someone is making or has made while executing the process. For example, a student demonstrates error analysis of the mental skill of adding fractions by identifying and describing mistakes that someone has made in carrying out this procedure. A question that would elicit this type of thinking is:

John has added two thirds and three fourths and come up with five sevenths. Describe the errors he has made in his computation.

A question that would elicit error analysis relative to the mental process of using the word- processing software WordPerfect is:

Robert plans to perform the following steps to write a composition using WordPerfect. Identify what will go wrong if he carries out the following steps exactly as stated:

1. When he gets into WordPerfect, he will begin by clicking on the CENTER command on the bar at the top of the page.

2. He will type in his three-paragraph composition.

3. When he is done, he will click on the small x in the upper right-hand corner of the screen.

4. The next day he will reopen WordPerfect and print out his composition.

Error analysis for psychomotor procedures is basically identical to error analysis for mental procedures. It involves the identification of errors someone has made or is making while carrying out the skill or process. A task that would elicit error analysis relative to a psychomotor skill is:

I am going to demonstrate the backhand stroke in tennis, but I'm going to make some mistakes. Describe what I am doing incorrectly and the effects these errors will have.

A task that would elicit error analysis relative to a psychomotor process is:

Shortly you will see a brief videotape of a woman returning serves in tennis. Describe the errors she is making and the effects they are having.

Generalizing

The analysis skill of generalizing involves inferring new generalizations and principles from information that is known. Figure 5.11 lists generalizing objectives across the three knowledge domains.

As it relates to details, generalizing involves inferring generalizations and principles from such specific elements as terms, facts, or events. For example, a student demonstrates the analytic skill of generalizing relative to a detail by constructing a generalization or principle about the nature of political assas-

Information		
	Details	The student can construct and defend new generalizations and principles based on known details.
	Organizing Ideas	The student can construct and defend new generalizations and principles based on known generalizations or principles.
Mental Procedures		
	Skills	The student can construct and defend new generalizations and principles based on information about specific mental skills.
	Processes	The student can construct and defend new generalizations and principles based on information about specific mental processes.
Psychomotor Procedures		
	Skills	The student can construct and defend new generalizations and principles based on information about specific psychomotor skills.
	Processes	The student can construct and defend new generalizations and principles based on information about specific psychomotor processes.

Figure 5.11. Generalizing Objectives

sinations based on specific events that have been addressed in class. A question that would elicit this type of thinking is:

> We have been studying a number of political assassinations that have occurred. Based on these examples, what generalizations can you make about political assassinations? Be sure to provide evidence for your conclusions.

Generalizing is a fairly sophisticated skill as it relates to organizing ideas. It involves the articulation of new generalizations and principles based on known generalizations and principles. For example, a student demonstrates generalizing as it relates to organizing ideas by constructing a new conclusion about life on earth based on a set of related principles and generalizations. A question that would elicit this type of thinking is:

Below is a set of statements we have been studying about life on earth. What are some conclusions you might come to that are supported by these generalizations? Explain your reasoning.

- There have been profound changes in the climate over the earth.
- Coordination and integration of action is generally slower in plants than in animals.
- There is an increasing complexity of structure and function from lower to higher forms of life.
- All life comes from life and produces its own kind of living organism.
- Light is a limiting factor of life.

Generalizing, as it relates to mental skills, involves constructing and defending conclusions about a set of skills. For example, students demonstrate generalizing when they generate a new conclusion about reading charts and graphs in general from their understanding of the skills involved in reading particular types of charts and graphs. A question that would elicit this type of thinking is:

What generalization or conclusion can you infer about reading charts and graphs in general from your understanding of the steps involved in reading the following types of charts and graphs: bar graphs, pie charts, histograms, line graphs? What specific information did you use to infer your conclusion and how does that information support your conclusion?

Generalizing as it relates to processes is similar to generalization as it relates to skills. Students infer new conclusions based on their understanding of two or more processes. A question that would elicit this type of thinking is:

What conclusions can you infer about the process of composing in general based on your understanding of the following: the process of painting a picture, the process of writing a song, the process of writing a story? What specific information did you use to generate this new conclusion?

Psychomotor procedures follow the same pattern as mental procedures. A question that would elicit generalizing as it relates to psychomotor skills is:

What general conclusion can you infer about batting, based on your understanding of the following skills:

- Hitting a curve ball

- Hitting a fast ball
- Hitting a knuckle ball
- Hitting a slider

A question that would elicit generalization relative to psychomotor processes is:

What general conclusion can you infer about the process of throwing, based on your understanding of the following:

- Throwing a baseball
- Throwing a javelin
- Throwing a discus
- Throwing a shot put

Specifying

The analysis skill of specifying involves making and defending predictions about what might happen or what will necessarily happen in a given situation. Figure 5.12 lists objectives for specifying across the three knowledge domains.

As depicted in Figure 5.12, specifying does not apply to details, because details are inherently too specific to involve rules from which predictions can be made. On the other hand, specifying is a natural type of thinking relative to organizing ideas which, by definition, are rule based.

Specifying, as it relates to generalizations, involves identifying what might be or must be true about a specific item based on an understanding of the class or category to which that item belongs. For example, a student demonstrates knowledge specification by generating and defending statements about what must be true about a specific type of bear given his or her knowledge of bears in general. A question that would elicit this type of thinking is:

A new species of bear has been discovered in Alaska. Given that it is a type of Alaskan bear, what are some characteristics it must possess and some characteristics it might possess? On what basis did you identify those characteristics that it must possess versus those characteristics it might possess?

Specifying as it relates to principles involves making and defending predictions about what will or might happen under certain conditions. For example, a student is involved in the process of specifying by identifying what must happen or what might happen if the earth's orbit were a circle as opposed to an ellipse. A question that would elicit this type of thinking is:

Information	
Details	NA
Organizing Ideas	The student can identify characteristics that might be true or must be true under certain conditions relative to a given generalization. The student can make and defend predictions about what might happen or must happen under certain conditions relative to a given principle.
Mental Procedures	
Skills	The student can make and defend inferences about what might happen or must happen under specific conditions relative to a mental skill.
Processes	The student can make and defend inferences about what might happen or must happen under specific conditions relative to a mental process.
Psychomotor Procedures	
Skills	The student can make and defend inferences about what might happen or must happen under certain conditions relative to a psychomotor skill.
Processes	The student can make and defend inferences about what might happen or must happen under certain conditions relative to a psychomotor process.

Figure 5.12. Specifying Objectives

We know that the earth's orbit is elliptical and that there are certain things that happen on earth as a result. Assume, though, that the earth's orbit was a circle. What are some things that would necessarily change and what are some things that might change? Explain the reasoning behind your predictions.

Specifying, as it relates to mental skills and processes, involves identifying what must happen or might happen during the execution of the skill or process under specific conditions. For example, a student demonstrates knowledge specification by determining how the procedure of reading a bar graph would be altered if no legend was provided. A question that would elicit this type of thinking is:

How would you have to modify the process of reading a bar graph if no title was provided? Explain why your modifications are necessary.

A question that would elicit knowledge specification relative to the mental process of writing is:

How would you have to modify the process of writing if you could not write multiple drafts? Explain why the modifications are necessary.

Specifying as it relates to psychomotor procedures is the same as specifying as it relates to mental procedures—students identify what must happen or might happen in the execution of a procedure under certain conditions. A question that would elicit specifying relative to a psychomotor skill is:

Describe what would happen during a roundhouse kick in karate if the first movement you make when executing this kick is to raise the knee of your kicking leg as high as possible to your chest.

A question that would elicit specifying relative to a psychomotor process is:

Explain how you would have to modify your batting stance and batting technique to accommodate a pitcher who can throw a fastball 110 miles per hour.

Level 4: Knowledge Utilization

As the name implies, the knowledge utilization processes require that students apply or use knowledge in specific situations. In such cases, the student's mental activity is not focused on the knowledge per se (as is the case with the analysis processes). Rather, the student's mental activity is focused on a specific situation that is enhanced as a result of the knowledge. For example, while Jane is engaged in the analytic process of error analysis relative to a principle about barometric pressure, her focus is on the information about barometric pressure. However, if she were using her knowledge of barometric pressure to help make a decision (a knowledge utilization process) about whether to stage a party indoors or outdoors, her focus would be on the party as opposed to barometric pressure per se.

There are four knowledge application processes: (1) decision making, (2) problem solving, (3) experimental inquiry, and (4) investigation. We consider each.

Information	
Details	The student can use his or her knowledge of details to make a specific decision.
Organizing Ideas	The student uses his or her knowledge of a generalization or principle to make specific decisions.

Mental Procedures	
Skills	The student can use his or her skill at or knowledge of a mental skill to make specific decisions.
Processes	The student can use his or her skill at or knowledge of a mental process to make a specific decision.

Psychomotor Procedures	
Skills	The student can use his or her skill at or knowledge of a psychomotor skill to make a specific decision.
Processes	The student can use his or her skill at or knowledge of a psychomotor process to make a specific decision.

Figure 5.13. Decision-Making Objectives

Decision Making

Decision making involves selecting among alternatives that initially appear equal. Figure 5.13 lists decision-making objectives across the three knowledge domains.

Details are frequently employed as critical components in decisions. For example, students demonstrate the use of details to make decisions when they use their knowledge of specific locations to determine the best site for a waste disposal plant. The following question would elicit this type of thinking:

Assume that the following three sites are being considered as the location for a new waste disposal plant: (1) near the lake at the north end of town, (2) near the airport, and (3) in the mountains outside town. Which site would be best? Explain why the specific characteristics of the site you selected make it the best selection.

Generalizations and principles are invariably key components of the decision-making process. Consider the example above. It is true that details about the three locations are used to make the decision. However, it is also necessary to use generalizations or principles about waste disposal plants.

Organizing ideas, then, are generally the criteria one uses to make selections between alternatives. A decision-making task that would highlight the use of organizing ideas is:

> Your job is to determine who among the following individuals would be the best peacetime leader: (a) Martin Luther King, Jr., (b) Anwar Sadat, or (c) Franklin D. Roosevelt. Explain the criteria you used to select among the three.

To select among these alternatives, the student must use some form of organizing ideas— probably generalizations—about peacetime leaders like the following:

Peacetime leaders should have a good understanding of similarities and differences between cultures.

Mental skills are sometimes used as explicit tools with which to gather information for decisions. For example, to elicit decision making that necessarily employs a specific mental skill, a student might be presented with a decision-making task like that below:

> Using the contour map of the region known as Four Corners, identify the best location to locate a water purification plant. Be sure to explain how the information in the contour map allowed you to select the best alternative.

Note that the directions to the task ask students to explain how the information in the contour map is useful in making the decision. Directions such as these are probably necessary to highlight the central role of a specific mental skill.

A task that would elicit the use of a specific mental process to make a decision is:

> Using the statistical program Ecostat as a tool, decide which of the three stocks we have been following in class would be the best long-term investment. Explain how the computer program aided in making this decision.

Psychomotor skills and processes can be used when making decisions. However, the types of decisions in which they can be employed are somewhat restricted. Most commonly, the decision involves the best skill or process to use in a specific situation. For example, below is a decision-making task that involves specific karate skills:

> Which is the best kick to use against an opponent who has a strong front kick and side kick, but a weak roundhouse kick?

A decision-making task that would make use of psychomotor processes is:

Identify which of the following processes is the best for you to rely on to win a point in tennis against a strong opponent:

1. Your ability to return a serve

2. Your ability to volley

3. Your ability to play the net

Problem Solving

The knowledge utilization process of problem solving involves accomplishing a goal for which obstacles or limiting conditions exist. Figure 5.14 lists problem-solving objectives across the three knowledge domains.

Problem solving is closely related to decision making in that the latter is frequently a subcomponent of problem solving. However, whereas decision making does not involve obstacles to a goal, problem solving does.

Knowledge of details is commonly necessary to solve problems. For example, students might use their knowledge about a specific Broadway musical to help solve a problem in its staging. To illustrate, consider the following task:

You are putting on the play, *Guys and Dolls*, but have no money to build a set. In fact, you can use only boxes as the materials for your set. Draw a sketch of how you would stage a particular scene and explain how your use of the boxes is called for by that scene.

Within this task, it is a student's knowledge of a specific scene (i.e., a specific detail) within *Guys and Dolls* that provides the logic for stage design using boxes only.

Organizing ideas apply to a variety of problem-solving tasks. Commonly, a student uses a generalization or principle when identifying how best to overcome the obstacle within the problem. To illustrate, reconsider the problem about staging the musical *Guys and Dolls*. It can be easily restated so as to emphasize a theatrical principle:

You are putting on the play, *Guys and Dolls*, but have no money to build a set. In fact, you can use only boxes as your staging materials. Draw a sketch of how you would stage a particular scene. Explain how your use of the boxes is based on specific principles of set design.

The tool used to solve this problem is a specific principle or principles about set design as opposed to details about the musical.

Information	
Details	The student can use his or her knowledge of details to solve a specific problem.
Organizing Ideas	The student can use his or her knowledge of a generalization or principle to help solve a specific problem.
Mental Procedures	
Skills	The student can use his or her skill at or understanding of a mental skill to solve a specific problem.
Processes	The student can use his or her skill at or understanding of a mental process to solve a specific problem.
Psychomotor Procedures	
Skills	The student can use his or her skill at or understanding of a psychomotor skill to solve a specific problem.
Processes	The student can use his or her skill at or understanding of a psychomotor process to solve a specific problem.

Figure 5.14. Problem-Solving Objectives

Specific mental skills can be vital to solving problems. For example, the following tasks require students to use the skills of mental computation and estimation:

> Your job is to build a fence that encompasses the largest span with 1,000 feet of two-by-four-inch planks. You must perform all computations and estimations mentally. That is, you may not use a calculator or keep track of your calculations using paper and pencil. Explain how the use of estimation and mental computation affected your ability to solve this problem.

Note that the directions of the problem ask students to explain how the use of specific mental skills—in this case estimation and mental computation—affect the problem-solving process.

Mental processes are frequently tools that are essential to solving a given problem. For example, the process of using a specific type of computer spreadsheet might be an integral aspect of overcoming a constraint in a given problem. Again, a task must be structured so as to make the process an integral part:

> You have been supplied with a table that shows the following for a company you own: sales per week, unit price for production of new products, cash reserve in the bank, and overhead expenses broken down by various categories. Your job is to design a strategy to increase cash flow as much as possible in a 6-month period. However, you cannot decrease or increase any of these variables by any more than 5% over the 6-month period. You must use the spreadsheet program Excel that we have been studying. When you are done, explain how the use of Excel was involved in finding a solution to this problem.

Psychomotor skills and processes or knowledge of psychomotor skills and processes is used to solve problems that are fundamentally physical in nature. For example, a student might use his or her skill at serving to solve a problem in tennis:

> You are going to play a match against someone who has exceptionally good ground strokes—backhand and forehand. In addition, you will be unable to use your forehand very much. What is your strategy?

The following task employs the use of psychomotor processes from the sport of basketball to solve a problem specific to basketball:

> Your technique for guarding an opponent relies heavily on quick, lateral (side-to-side) movement on your part. However, you have pulled a muscle in such a way that it makes it difficult for you to move quickly to your right. What will you do to effectively guard an opponent who is your equal in terms of quickness but can't jump as high as you can?

Experimental Inquiry

Experimental inquiry involves the generation and testing of hypotheses about a specific physical or psychological phenomenon. Figure 5.15 lists experimental inquiry objectives across the three knowledge domains.

Details are sometimes used as the basis for hypothesis generation and testing. For example, a knowledge of details about the transportation system in a specific city might be used by a student to generate and test hypotheses about that system. A question that would elicit this type of thinking is:

Information		
	Details	The student can use his or her knowledge of details to generate and test hypotheses.
	Organizing Ideas	The student can use his or her knowledge of a generalization or principle to generate and test hypotheses.
Mental Procedures		
	Skills	The student can use his or her skill at or understanding of a mental skill to generate and test hypotheses.
	Processes	The student can use his or her skill at or understanding of a mental process to generate and test hypotheses.
Psychomotor Procedures		
	Skills	The student can use his or her skill at or knowledge of a psychomotor skill to generate and test an hypothesis.
	Processes	The student can use his or her knowledge of or skill at a psychomotor process to generate and test a hypothesis.

Figure 5.15. Experimental Inquiry Objectives

We have been studying the public transportation system for the city of Denver. Using these facts, generate and test a hypothesis about some aspect of that system.

Experimental inquiry is particularly well suited to organizing ideas since these knowledge structures most readily lend themselves to hypothesis generation. For example, Peter, a psychology student, might use his understanding of a principle about how people react to certain types of information to generate and test a hypothesis about the reactions of his peers to a specific type of advertisement. A task that would elicit this type of thinking is:

We have been studying principles concerning how human beings react to certain types of information. Select one of these principles, then make a prediction about how your classmates would react to a specific type of advertisement. Be sure to explain the logic behind your predictions. Carry out an activity to test your prediction and explain whether the results confirm or disconfirm your original hypothesis.

Mental skills and processes are sometimes necessary tools used in the generation and testing of hypotheses. For example, use of the mental skill of reading the periodic table might be an integral part of an experimental inquiry task:

Using the periodic table, generate a hypothesis about the interaction of two or more elements. Then, carry out an activity that tests the hypothesis. Report and explain your findings.

The following task would use the mental process of accessing the World Wide Web as a tool in experimental inquiry:

Using the World Wide Web as your source of information, generate and test a hypothesis about the types of Web sites that are developed by specific types of organizations.

In certain situations, psychomotor skills and processes may be used as tools in experimental inquiry. The following is an experimental inquiry task that involves students' understanding of the psychomotor skill of hitting a wedge shot in golf:

Generate and test a hypothesis about the use of a sand wedge in a situation where your golf ball rests on flat, hardened sand.

A task that involves the psychomotor process of charging the net in tennis as a tool in experimental inquiry is:

Using the technique of charging the net as your tool for gathering information, generate and test a hypothesis about playing a specific type of opponent.

Investigation

Investigation involves examining a past, present, or future situation. As explained in Chapter 4, it can be likened to experimental inquiry in that it involves hypothesis generation and testing. However, the data used are not gathered by direct observation. Rather, the data are assertions and opinions that have been stated by others. In addition, the rules of evidence are different from those employed in experimental inquiry. Figure 5.16 lists the manner in which the knowledge utilization process of investigation applies across the knowledge domains.

A knowledge of specific details is commonly the impetus for an investigation. For example, a student's understanding of details surrounding the assas-

Information		
Details	The student can use his or her knowledge of specific details to investigate a past, present, or future event.	
Organizing Ideas	The student can use his or her knowledge of a generalization or principle to investigate a past, present, or future event.	
Mental Procedures		
Skills	The student can use his or her skill at or knowledge of a mental skill as a tool to investigate a past, present, or future event.	
Processes	The student can use his or her skill at or knowledge of a mental process as a tool to investigate a past, present, or future event.	
Psychomotor Procedures		
Skills	NA	
Processes	NA	

Figure 5.16. Investigation Objectives

sination of John F. Kennedy might stimulate the student to find out what actually occurred. A task that would stimulate this form of investigation is:

> We have been studying the 1963 assassination of John F. Kennedy. There are a number of conflicting accounts. Identify one of the conflicting accounts of this incident and investigate what is known about it.

Organizing ideas are very commonly the basis for investigations. For example, a student's understanding of a principle about the relationship between polar ice caps and ocean depth might be used as the basis for an investigation task like the following:

> We have been studying the relationship between ocean depth and polar ice caps. Using your knowledge of these principles, investigate what might happen if the earth's temperature were to rise by 5 degrees over the next three decades.

Mental skills are sometimes used as direct tools in investigations. For example, the skill of reading a specific type of map might be critical to a given investigation.

Below is a contour map of Colorado in the year 1900. Use the information on the map as the basis for investigating why Denver became the largest city in the state.

Like mental skills, mental processes are sometimes used as tools in investigations. For example, the process of using a specific type of Internet database might be a tool necessary to an investigation task like the following:

We have been using an Internet database that contains eyewitness stories from more than 5,000 survivors of the Holocaust. Using that database, investigate what you consider to be accurate and inaccurate accounts about what happened at Auschwitz during World War II.

It is difficult to employ psychomotor skills processes as tools in an investigation task. This is so because these procedures do not lend themselves to gathering or examining assertions or opinions of others. As we have seen, these are the data by which hypotheses are tested in investigation.

Level 5: Metacognition

As described in Chapter 3, there are four categories of metacognitive processes: (1) goal setting, (2) process monitoring, (3) monitoring clarity, and (4) monitoring accuracy.

Goal Setting

The metacognitive process of goal setting involves setting specific goals relative to one's understanding of or skill at a specific type of knowledge. Figure 5.17 lists goal setting objectives across the three knowledge domains.

As depicted in Figure 5.17, goal setting not only involves setting goals for specific types of knowledge, but it also involves identifying how those goals might be accomplished. To demonstrate goal setting, then, a student must not only articulate a goal relative to a specific knowledge component, but also identify the specifics of a plan to accomplish the goal.

Questions that would elicit this type of metacognitive processing include

Details: What is a goal you have or might have relative to your understanding of the 1999 conflict in Kosovo? What would you have to do to accomplish this goal?

Information		
Details	The student can set and plan for goals relative to his or her knowledge of specific details.
Organizing Ideas	The student can set and plan for goals relative to his or her knowledge of specific generalizations and principles.
Mental Procedures		
Skills	The student can set and plan for goals relative to his or her competence in a specific mental skill.
Processes	The student can set and plan for goals relative to his or her competence in a specific mental process.
Psychomotor Procedures		
Skills	The student can set and plan for goals relative to his or her competence in a specific psychomotor skill.
Processes	The student can set and plan for goals relative to his or her competence in a specific psychomotor process.

Figure 5.17. Goal-Setting Objectives

Organizing ideas: What is a goal you have or might have relative to your understanding of Bernoulli's principle? How might you accomplish this goal?

Mental skills: What is a goal you have or might have relative to your ability to read a contour map? What would you have to do to accomplish this goal?

Mental processes: What is a goal you have or might have relative to your ability to use WordPerfect? How might you accomplish this goal?

Psychomotor skills: What is a goal you have or might have relative to your skill at making a backhand shot? What would you have to do to accomplish this goal?

Psychomotor Processes: What is a goal you have or might have relative to your ability to play defense in basketball? How would you accomplish this goal?

It is the student's response to the question regarding the manner in which the goal will be accomplished that provides insight into the level at which a student is employing the metacognitive process of goal setting. For example, a response in which the student notes that "I will have to work harder" to accomplish this goal does not truly address the metacognitive process of goal setting. Rather, the student should identify a clear objective, a rough time line, necessary resources, and the like.

Process Monitoring

Process monitoring involves determining how effectively a procedure is being carried out in real time. For example, Sally is involved in process monitoring if, while playing defense in basketball, she continually determines which of her actions are effective, which are not, and what she might do to improve her effectiveness.

Process monitoring objectives are stated in Figure 5.18 for the three knowledge domains.

As Figure 5.18 indicates, process monitoring applies to the two procedural knowledge domains only—mental procedures and psychomotor procedures. This is so because process monitoring, by definition, relates only to knowledge that can be executed. As discussed in Chapter 3, informational knowledge (details and organizing ideas) is not subject to execution. It can be recalled, but it is not "carried out" as is procedural knowledge.

To elicit process monitoring in students, tasks must be designed in such a way that students can think about and monitor a skill or process while engaged in its execution. Commonly, situations must be contrived so that a student can execute the procedure but also have the opportunity to comment on its execution.

Questions which would elicit process monitoring include

Mental skills: Below are four problems that involve transforming fractions to ratios. As you solve these problems, describe how effective you are at performing this transformation, paying particular attention to those things you must change to be more effective.

Mental processes: Your task is to write a short letter, save the letter on your hard drive, then print it out using letterhead paper. All this is to be done using WordPerfect. As you do this, describe how effective you are at using WordPerfect, paying particular attention to those things you should change to be more effective.

Psychomotor skills: Demonstrate the proper technique for stretching the hamstring muscles. As you do so, identify and describe how effectively you think you are executing this skill.

Psychomotor process: In a moment you will be asked to play defense against another basketball opponent. However, periodically we will

Information		
Details	NA	
Organizing Ideas	NA	
Mental Procedures		
Skills	The student can monitor the extent to which a specific mental skill is being executed effectively.	
Processes	The student can monitor the extent to which a specific mental process is being executed effectively.	
Psychomotor Procedures		
Skills	The student can monitor the extent to which a specific psychomotor skill is being executed effectively.	
Processes	The student can monitor the extent to which a specific psychomotor process is being executed effectively.	

Figure 5.18. Process-Monitoring Objectives

stop the action and ask you to describe how effectively you think you are playing defense, paying particular attention to what you might do to improve.

Monitoring Clarity

As its name implies, monitoring clarity involves determining the extent to which an individual is clear about specific aspects of knowledge. Clarity is defined here as being free from indistinction or ambiguity. Stated in more positive terms, one who is clear about knowledge can recognize the distinctions important to that knowledge and ascribe precise meaning to each important distinction. For example, a student who has clarity about the concept of "central tendency" knows that the mean, median, and mode are different descriptions of central tendency and understands the meaning of each of these types. Figure 5.19 lists objectives for monitoring clarity across the three knowledge domains.

As Figure 5.19 indicates, the metacognitive process of monitoring clarity applies to all three knowledge domains in approximately the same way. Questions like the following can be used to stimulate this type of metacognitive thinking:

Information	
Details	The student can identify those aspects of details about which he or she has difficulty making distinctions or is ambiguous.
Organizing Ideas	The student can identify those aspects of a generalization or principle about which he or she has difficulty making distinctions or is ambiguous.
Mental Procedures	
Skills	The student can identify those aspects of a mental skill about which he or she has difficulty making distinctions or is ambiguous.
Processes	The student can identify those aspects of a mental process about which he or she has difficulty making distinctions or is ambiguous.
Psychomotor Procedures	
Skills	The student can identify those aspects of a psychomotor skill about which he or she has difficulty making distinctions or is ambiguous.
Processes	The student can identify those aspects of a psychomotor process about which he or she has difficulty making distinctions or is ambiguous.

Figure 5.19. Monitoring Clarity Objectives

Details: Identify those things about the 1999 conflict in Kosovo about which you are confused. What do you think is causing your confusion?

Organizing ideas: Identify those aspects of Bernoulli's principle about which you are confused. Be specific about those areas of confusion. What don't you understand?

Mental skill: Identify those parts of the skill of reading a contour map about which you are confused. What do you think is causing your confusion?

Mental process: Identify those aspects of the process of using the word processing program WordPerfect about which you are confused. Be as specific as you can.

Psychomotor skill: Identify those parts of the technique for stretching the hamstring muscles about which you are confused. What do you think is causing your confusion?

Psychomotor process: Identify those aspects of playing defense in basketball about which you are confused. What are the causes of your confusion? Be as specific as possible.

The more precise students can be about their areas of lack of clarity, the more they are exercising the metacognitive process of monitoring clarity. For example, one level of monitoring for clarity regarding the mental process of using WordPerfect would be demonstrated by a student response like the following:

"I get confused when I try to center things."

However, a much deeper level of metacognitive awareness would be exhibited by the following response:

"I don't understand how you can go back and center a line in the middle of a document without losing all the margins that you have already set up."

Monitoring Accuracy

Monitoring accuracy involves determining the extent to which one is correct in terms of one's understanding of specific knowledge. Monitoring accuracy is distinct from, but related to, monitoring clarity. That is, a student could be clear about some aspects of knowledge—have no ambiguity or lack of distinction—but, in fact, be inaccurate. Figure 5.20 lists objectives for monitoring accuracy across the three knowledge domains.

As Figure 5.20 illustrates, a critical aspect of monitoring accuracy is defending or verifying one's judgment of accuracy. This implies that students must not only make a judgment about their accuracy, but must provide evidence for this judgment: They must reference some outside source as proof of their assessment of accuracy.

Questions that elicit this type of metacognitive processing include

Details: Identify those aspects about the 1999 conflict in Kosovo about which you are sure you are accurate and then explain how you know you are accurate. What is the evidence for your judgment of accuracy?

Organizing ideas: Identify those aspects of Bernoulli's principle about which you are sure you are correct. What is the evidence for your judgment of accuracy?

Mental skill: Identify those aspects of the skill of reading a contour map about which you are sure you are accurate. What evidence do you have for your judgment of accuracy?

Mental process: Identify those aspects of using WordPerfect about which you are sure you are correct. What is the evidence for your judgment of accuracy?

Information		
	Details	The student can identify and defend the extent to which he or she is correct about his or her knowledge of specific details.
	Organizing Ideas	The student can identify and defend the extent to which he or she is correct about his or her understanding of a specific generalization or principle.
Mental Procedures		
	Skills	The student can identify and defend the extent to which he or she is correct about his or her understanding of a mental skill.
	Processes	The student can identify and defend the extent to which he or she is correct about his or her understanding of a mental process.
Psychomotor Procedures		
	Skill	The student can identify and defend the extent to which he or she is correct about his or her understanding of a psychomotor skill.
	Processes	The student can identify and defend the extent to which he or she is correct about his or her understanding of a psychomotor process.

Figure 5.20. Monitoring Accuracy Objectives

Psychomotor skill: Identify those aspects of the process of stretching the hamstrings about which you are sure you are accurate. What is your evidence for your judgment of accuracy?

Psychomotor Process: Identify those aspects of playing defense in basketball about which you are sure you are correct. What evidence do you have for your judgment?

Level 6: Self-System Thinking

As described in Chapter 4, self-system thinking involves four aspects: (1) examining importance, (2) examining efficacy, (3) examining emotional response, and (4) examining motivation.

Information		
Details	The student can identify the personal importance he or she places on details and analyze the reasoning behind his or her judgments.
Organizing Ideas	The student can identify the personal importance he or she places on a generalization or principle and analyze the reasoning behind his or her judgments.

Mental Procedures		
Skills	The student can identify the personal importance he or she places on a mental skill and analyze the reasoning behind his or her judgments.
Processes	The student can identify the personal importance he or she places on a mental process and analyze the reasoning behind his or her judgments.

Psychomotor Procedures		
Skills	The student can identify the personal importance he or she places on a psychomotor skill and analyze the reasoning behind his or her judgments.
Processes	The student can identify the personal importance he or she places on a psychomotor process and analyze the reasoning behind his or her judgments.

Figure 5.21. Examining Importance Objectives

Examining Importance

The self-system process of examining importance involves analyzing the extent to which one believes that specific knowledge is important. As explained in Chapter 4, if an individual does not perceive a specific piece of knowledge important at a personal level, he will probably not be highly motivated to learn it.

Figure 5.21 lists objectives for the self-system process of examining importance across the three knowledge domains.

As depicted in Figure 5.21, the process of examining importance is fundamentally identical across the knowledge domains. This type of self-system thinking can be elicited by fairly direct questions like the following:

Details: How important do you think it is for you to have a knowledge of the events surrounding the assassination of John F. Kennedy in 1963? Why do you believe this and how logical is your thinking?

Organizing ideas: How important do you believe it is for you to have an understanding of Bernoulli's principle? Why do you believe this and how valid is your thinking?

Mental skills: How important do you believe it is for you to be able to read a contour map? Why do you believe this, and how logical is your thinking?

Mental processes: How important do you believe it is for you to be able to use WordPerfect? Why do you believe this and how valid is your thinking?

Psychomotor skills: How important do you believe it is for you to be able to effectively stretch the hamstring muscles? Why do you believe this and how logical is your thinking?

Psychomotor processes: How important do you believe it is for you to be able to effectively play defense in basketball? Why do you believe this and how valid is your thinking?

It is the students' response to the two-part "tag question" illustrated above that provides the greatest insight into their ability to engage in this type of self-system thinking. That is, to effectively engage in the process of analyzing importance, students must not only be able to explain the reasoning behind why they believe something is important or unimportant, but they must also be able to examine the reasonableness or logic of these judgments.

Examining Efficacy

The self-system process of examining efficacy involves examining the extent to which individuals believe they can improve their understanding or competence relative to a specific type of knowledge. As explained in Chapter 4, if individuals do not believe they can change their competence relative to a specific piece of knowledge, they will probably not be motivated to learn it even if they perceive it as important. Figure 5.22 lists objectives for examining efficacy across the three knowledge domains.

Again, it is not just the ability to identify the beliefs that underlie a student's perceptions, but it is also the student's ability to analyze the validity or logic of these beliefs that demonstrates this type of self-system thinking. Questions that would stimulate this type of thinking relative to the three knowledge domains include

Information	
Details	The student can identify the extent to which he or she believes his or her understanding of a specific detail can be improved and analyze the reasoning behind these beliefs.
Organizing Ideas	The student can identify the extent to which he or she believes his or her understanding of a generalization or principle can be improved and analyze the reasoning behind these beliefs.
Mental Procedures	
Skills	The student can identify the extent to which he or she believes his or her competence at a mental skill can be improved and analyze the reasoning behind these beliefs.
Processes	The student can identify the extent to which he or she believes his or her competence at a mental process can be improved and analyze the reasoning behind these beliefs.
Psychomotor Procedures	
Skills	The student can identify the extent to which he or she believes his or her competence at a psychomotor skill can be improved and analyze the reasoning behind these beliefs.
Processes	The student can identify the extent to which he or she believes his or her competence at a psychomotor process can be improved and analyze the reasoning behind these beliefs.

Figure 5.22. Examining Efficacy Objectives

Details: To what extent do you believe you can improve your understanding of the John F. Kennedy assassination? What is the reasoning underlying this belief, and how logical is your thinking?

Organizing ideas: To what extent do you believe you can improve your understanding of Bernoulli's principle? Why do you believe this? How reasonable is your thinking?

Mental skills: To what extent do you believe you can improve your ability to read a contour map? What is the reasoning behind this belief, and how logical is your thinking?

Mental processes: To what extent do you believe you can improve your ability to use WordPerfect? Why do you believe this? How reasonable is your thinking?

Psychomotor skills: To what extent do you think you can improve your skill at making a backhand shot? What is the reasoning behind this belief, and how logical is your thinking?

Psychomotor processes: To what extent do you think you can improve your skill at playing defense in basketball? Why do you believe this? How reasonable is your thinking?

Examining Emotional Response

The process of examining emotional response involves identifying what emotions, if any, are associated with specific knowledge and why those associations exist. As described in Chapter 4, negative affect can dampen a student's motivation to learn or improve at something even if the student believes that it is important and that he has the requisite ability and resources.

Figure 5.23 lists objectives for examining emotional response across the three knowledge domains.

Questions that would elicit this type of self-system thinking in students include

Details: What, if any, emotions do you have associated with the conflict in Kosovo? What is the thinking behind these associations? How logical is this thinking?

Organizing ideas: What emotions, if any, do you associate with Bernoulli's principle? What is your thinking behind these associations? How reasonable is your thinking?

Mental skills: What emotions, if any, do you associate with the skill of reading a contour map? What is your thinking behind these associations? How logical are these associations?

Mental processes: What emotions, if any, do you associate with the use of WordPerfect? What is your thinking behind these associations? How logical is your thinking?

Psychomotor skills: What emotions, if any do you associate with the technique for making a backhand shot? What is your thinking behind these associations? How reasonable is your thinking?

Psychomotor processes: What emotions, if any, do you associate with playing defense in basketball? What is your thinking behind these associations? How logical is your thinking?

Information		
	Details	The student can identify any emotions associated with specific details and analyze the reasoning behind these associations.
	Organizing Ideas	The student can identify any emotions associated with a generalization or principle and analyze the reasoning behind these associations.
Mental Procedures		
	Skills	The student can identify any emotions associated with a mental skill and the reasoning behind these associations.
	Processes	The student can identify any emotions associated with a mental process and the reasoning behind these associations.
Psychomotor Procedures		
	Skills	The student can identify any emotions associated with a psychomotor skill and analyze the reasoning behind these associations.
	Processes	The student can identify any emotions associated with a psychomotor process and analyze the reasoning behind these associations.

Figure 5.23. Emotional Response Objectives

The key feature of this type of self-system thinking is the identification of a pattern of thinking or experiences underlying a given association along with the reasonableness of this pattern of thinking. There is no necessary attempt to change these associations—only understand them. This said, an argument can be made that awareness of one's emotional associations provides the opportunity for some control over them.

Examining Motivation

The final type of self-system thinking involves examining overall motivation to improve one's understanding of or competence in a specific type of knowledge. As described in Chapter 4, overall motivation is a composition of the other three aspects of self-system thinking—perceptions of importance, perceptions of efficacy, and emotional response. Examining motivation, then,

Information		
Details	The student can identify his or her level of motivation to increase his or her understanding of specific details and analyze the reasoning for this level of motivation.	
Organizing Ideas	The student can identify his or her level of motivation to increase his or her understanding of a generalization or principle and analyze the reasoning for this level of motivation.	
Mental Procedures		
Skills	The student can identify his or her level of motivation to increase his or her competence in a mental skill and analyze the reasoning for this level of motivation.	
Processes	The student can identify his or her level of motivation to increase his or her competence in a mental process and analyze the reasoning for this level of motivation.	
Psychomotor Procedures		
Skills	The student can identify his or her level of motivation to increase his or her competence in a psychomotor skill and analyze the reasoning for this level of motivation.	
Processes	The student can identify his or her level of motivation to increase his or her competence in a psychomotor process and analyze the reasoning for this level of motivation.	

Figure 5.24. Examining Motivation Objectives

can be considered an "omnibus" self-system process incorporating the other three aspects of the self-system. Figure 5.24 lists objectives for examining motivation across the three knowledge domains.

Questions that would elicit this type of self-system thinking include

Details: How would you describe your level of motivation to increase your understanding of the conflict in Kosovo? What are your reasons for this level of motivation? How logical is your thinking?

Organizing ideas: How would you describe your level of motivation to increase your understanding of Bernoulli's principle? What are your reasons for this level of motivation? How valid are those reasons?

Mental skills: How would you describe your level of motivation to increase your ability to read a contour map? What are your reasons behind this level of motivation? How logical is your thinking?

Mental processes: How would you describe your level of motivation to increase your skill at using WordPerfect? What are your reasons for this level of motivation? How valid are those reasons?

Psychomotor skills: How would you describe your level of motivation to increase your competence at making a backhand shot? What are your reasons behind this level of motivation? How logical is your thinking?

Psychomotor processes: How would you describe your level of motivation to increase your skill at playing defense in basketball? What are the reasons behind this level of motivation? How logical is your thinking?

Ideally, when students respond to questions like those above, they consider all three self-system components that can affect motivation. That is, they comment on the importance they ascribe to the knowledge, the level of efficacy they perceive, and any emotions they associate with the knowledge. They also explain which of these three factors dominates their motivation.

Summary

In this chapter, the six levels of the New Taxonomy were described in terms of their relationship to the three knowledge domains—information, mental procedures, and psychomotor procedures. Objectives were stated for each knowledge type at each level along with questions and tasks that would elicit behavior with which each objective could be evaluated.

CHAPTER 6

Applying the Taxonomy

This chapter addresses the ways in which the New Taxonomy can be used by educators. Although there are a number of uses for the New Taxonomy, three seem obvious from the outset: (1) as a tool for designing educational objectives, (2) as a tool for designing spiral curriculums, and (3) as a tool for designing assessments.

Educational Outcomes

Certainly a primary use of the New Taxonomy is to provide a framework with which to design educational objectives. This was a primary motivation for the development of Bloom's Taxonomy. Indeed, a few years prior to the publication of Bloom's Taxonomy, Robert Travers, in a book titled *How to Make Achievement Tests,* lamented that a taxonomy of model processes was a prerequisite to the effective design of educational objectives.

> The basic difficulty in defining educational goals is due to the fact that psychologists have not yet developed a classification of human behavior which is useful for this purpose. A comprehensive taxonomy of human behavior which had a numerical value assigned to each category of behavior would simplify the educator's task. It would also provide teachers with a common language for discussing educational goals and ensure that those who used the same terms referred to the same concepts. (Travers, 1950, p. 10)

As mentioned in Chapter 1 of this text, the stated purpose of Bloom's Taxonomy was to meet this need. So, too, is the articulation of educational objectives a primary goal of the New Taxonomy.

It is important to note, though, that the New Taxonomy as described in this volume is not intended to prescribe the objectives that a school or district should adopt, only to articulate the range of possible objectives that a classroom teacher or an entire school or district might focus on, given an understanding of how the human mind operates. It is entirely possible that many or all of the elements inherent in the metacognitive and self-system processes might be considered beyond the purview of education within a given classroom, school, or district. In fact, it is reasonable to assume that some teachers, schools or districts might experience opposition to objectives that deal with the metacognitive and self-systems. To illustrate, E. D. Hirsch, popular advocate of what he refers to as the "core knowledge" curriculum, is highly critical of instructional objectives that deal with the metacognitive and self-systems. Hirsch gives four reasons why such objectives are problematic:

- [They] may interfere with the orderly development of adaptive problem-solving strategies.

- [They] may carry severe opportunity costs by usurping subject matter instruction.

- [They] may overload working memory and thus impair rather than help learning.

- All of these potential drawbacks may have the most adverse effects on slow or disadvantaged learners. (Hirsch, 1996, p. 139)

This said, there are compelling reasons why metacognitive and self-system learning objectives should be included in a comprehensive listing of objectives for a given type of knowledge. First, Hirsch fails to recognize the vast amount of research supporting the importance of metacognitive and self-system thinking to the learning process. Specifically, in their analysis of some 22,000 studies on 30 instructional variables, Wang, Haertel, and Walberg (1993) found that instructional strategies that focus on metacognitive and self-system processes were second in terms of their effect on student achievement (strategies that focus on classroom management had the greatest effect on student achievement).

Second, these areas seem to be systematically excluded from educational practice despite their importance in the learning process. This is particularly true of self-system objectives. For example, Garcia and her colleagues (Garcia & Pintrich, 1991, 1993; Pintrich & Garcia, 1992) note that the importance of the self-system in the learning process, although recognized by psychologists, has been virtually excluded from the instructional equation by educators.

Third, enhancing metacognitive and self-system thinking is central to developing self-regulation, which some psychologists assert should be a fundamental goal of education. As Bandura (1997) notes,

A fundamental goal of education is to equip students with self-regulatory capabilities that enable them to educate themselves. Self-directedness not only contributes to success in formal instruction, but also promotes lifelong learning. (p. 174)

Finally, there is growing evidence that the public at large is supportive of educational goals that address metacognitive and self-system thinking. To illustrate, in a study of public opinion as to which of 250 educational objectives were the most important for students to master prior to high school graduation, those rated in the top one third contained a significant proportion of objectives that were related to self-systems and metacognitive thinking. For example, the sixth-rated objective out of 250 was the ability to understand and maintain emotional health. (For a discussion, see Marzano, Kendall, & Cicchinelli, 1998; Marzano, Kendall, & Gaddy, 1999.)

Whether to include objectives, then, that address metacognitive and self-system thinking is a decision that must be made by individual teachers, schools, or districts. Certainly, not all content addressed during a unit of instruction is important enough to be addressed at all levels of the New Taxonomy. On the other hand, if educators wish students to address a given knowledge component as comprehensively as possible and/or wish to develop self-regulatory skills in students, then metacognitive and self-system objectives should be overtly addressed.

One final comment should be made about the use of the New Taxonomy as a framework for designing learning objectives. In Chapters 4 and 5, objectives have been stated in very general terms. Those familiar with the literature on instructional objectives will no doubt realize that some experts on learning objectives recommend that they take a specific form. For example, in his book, *Preparing Instructional Objectives*, Mager (1962) notes that a well-written instructional objective should include three elements:

1. Performance. An objective always says what a learner is expected to be able to do; the objective sometimes describes the product or result of the doing.

2. Conditions. An objective always describes the important conditions (if any) under which the performance is to occur.

3. Criterion. Whenever possible, an objective describes the criterion of acceptable performance by describing how well the learner must perform in order to be considered acceptable. (p. 21)

Even though the objectives based on the New Taxonomy have been stated in very general terms, they can easily be rewritten to meet Mager's specifications. To illustrate, consider the mental process of using WordPerfect. A general objective relative to the metacognitive skill of process monitoring would be:

Students can monitor the extent to which they are effectively carrying out the process of using WordPerfect.

Stated in terms that would more closely comply with Mager's criteria, this objective might read as follows:

> Given a one-paragraph letter already written, the student will type the letter in WordPerfect and store it on the hard drive. Exit WordPerfect; re-enter WordPerfect, then open the file in which the letter is stored and print it out on letterhead. While doing so, the student will identify any errors made in the process with 80% accuracy.

As a Structure for Designing a Spiral Curriculum

Another use of the New Taxonomy is to facilitate the design of a spiral curriculum. The concept of a spiral curriculum is one that has intrigued educators for decades. First popularized by curriculum reformer Hilda Taba (1967), the nature of a spiral curriculum was also addressed by Jerome Bruner (1960) and Patricia Murphy (1974). The fundamental principle underlying the concept of a spiral curriculum is that students should be introduced to new knowledge in its most rudimentary form. During subsequent encounters with the knowledge, however, more skill and depth of understanding should be expected.

What might be referred to as the "standards movement" in K-12 education can be viewed as an attempt to organize subject-matter content into a spiral curriculum. Although a complete discussion of the standard movement is beyond the scope of this text (for a detailed discussion see Marzano & Kendall, 1996a, 1996b), it is useful to briefly address the nature and function of that movement.

Many educators see the publication of the now-famous report, *A Nation at Risk* (National Commission on Excellence in Education, 1983), as the initiating event of the modern standards movement. Researcher Lorrie Shepard (1993) notes that, upon publication of the report, the rhetoric of education changed drastically. Proponents of reform began to make a close link between the financial security and economic competitiveness of the nation and our educational system. Who will soon forget the chilling words often quoted from *A Nation at Risk*: "The educational foundations of our society are presently being eroded by a rising tide of mediocrity that threatens our very future as a nation and a people. . . . We have, in effect been committing an act of unthinking, unilateral educational disarmament" (National Commission on Excellence in Education, 1983, p. 5).

These growing concerns about the educational preparation of the nation's youth prompted President Bush and the nation's governors to call an education summit in Charlottesville, Virginia, in September 1989. Shepard (1993) explains that at this summit, President Bush and the nation's governors, including then-governor Bill Clinton, agreed on six broad goals for education to be reached by the year 2000. These goals and the rationale for them are published under the title *The National Education Goals Report: Building a Nation of Learners* (National Education Goals Panel [NEGP], 1991). Two of those goals (3 and 4) relate specifically to academic achievement:

> Goal 3: By the year 2000, American students will leave grades 4, 8, and 12, having demonstrated competency in challenging subject matter, including English, mathematics, science, history, and geography; and every school in America will ensure that all students learn to use their minds well, so they may be prepared for responsible citizenship, further learning, and productive employment in our modern economy.

> Goal 4: By the year 2000, U.S. students will be first in the world in science and mathematics achievement.

As one of the tools for accomplishing these goals, standards for what students should know and be able to do were drafted in all the major subject areas. Figure 6.1 contains a listing of the standards documents identified by national subject-matter organizations.

In addition to the documents listed in Figure 6.1, 49 out of 50 states have identified state-level standards.

The common convention at the national and state levels is to define a standard as a general category of knowledge. For example, most national- and state-level documents identified a number of standards in science like those below:

Earth and Space

1. Understands basic features of the earth

2. Understands basic earth processes

3. Understands essential ideas about the composition and structure of the universe and Earth's place in it

Life Sciences

4. Knows about the diversity and unity that characterize life

5. Understands the genetic basis for the transfer of biological characteristics from one generation to the next

6. Knows the general structure and functions of cells in organisms

7. Understands how species depend on one another and on the environment for survival

8. Understands the cycling of matter and flow of energy through the living environment

9. Understands the basic concepts of the evolution of species

Science	National Research Council. (1996). *National Science Education Standards.* Washington, DC: National Academy Press.
Foreign Language	National Standards in Foreign Language Education Project. (1996). *Standards for Foreign Language Learning: Preparing for the 21st Century.* Lawrence, KS: Allen Press.
English Language Arts	National Council of Teachers of English and the International Reading Association. (1996). *Standards for the English Language Arts.* Urbana, IL: National Council of Teachers of English.
History	National Center for History in the Schools. (1994). *National Standards for History for Grades K-4: Expanding Children's World in Time and Space.* Los Angeles: Author. National Center for History in the Schools. (1994). *National Standards for United States History: Exploring the American Experience.* Los Angeles: Author. National Center for History in the Schools. (1994). *National Standards for World History: Exploring Paths to the Present.* Los Angeles: Author. National Center for History in the Schools. (1996). *National Standards for History: Basic Edition.* Los Angeles: Author.
Arts	Consortium of National Arts Education Associations. (1994). *National Standards for Arts Education: What Every Young American Should Know and Be Able to Do in the Arts.* Reston, VA: Music Educators National Conference.
Health	Joint Committee on National Health Education Standards. (1995). *National Health Education Standards: Achieving Health Literacy.* Reston, VA: Association for the Advancement of Health Education.
Civics	Center for Civic Education. (1994). *National Standards for Civics and Government.* Calabasas, CA: Author.
Economics	National Council on Economic Education. (1996, August).*Content Statements for State Standards in Economics, K-12* (unpublished manuscript). New York: Author.
Geography	Geography Education Standards Project. (1994). *Geography for Life: National Geography Standards.* Washington, DC: National Geographic Research and Exploration.
Physical Education	National Association for Sport and Physical Education. (1995). *Moving Into the Future, National Standards for Physical Education: A Guide to Content and Assessment.* St. Louis: Mosby.
Mathematics	National Council of Teachers of Mathematics. (1989). *Curriculum and Evaluation Standards for School Mathematics.* Reston, VA: Author.
Social Studies	National Council for the Social Studies. (1994). *Expectations of Excellence: Curriculum Standards for Social Studies.* Washington, DC: Author.

Figure 6.1. National Standards Document

Physical Sciences

10. Understands basic concepts about the structure and properties of matter

11. Understands energy types, sources, and conversions, and their relationship to heat and temperature

12. Understands motion and the principles that explain it

13. Knows the kinds of forces that exist between objects and within atoms

Science and Technology

14. Understands the nature of scientific knowledge

15. Understands the nature of scientific inquiry

16. Understands the scientific enterprise

17. Understands the nature of technological design

18. Understands the interactions of science, technology, and society

The content within each standard is then commonly further defined by more specific elements called benchmarks. Usually, multiple benchmarks are identified at grade-level intervals. For example, Figure 6.2 contains benchmarks at four grade level intervals (K-2, 3-5, 6-8, 9-12) for the standard titled, "Understands energy types, sources, and conversions and their relationship to heat and temperature." It is the sequencing of elements from level to level that defines the spiral curriculum.

Close inspection of Figure 6.2 illustrates that the criteria for the spiraling of content are rather weak. The most obvious difference from one level to the next is the quantity of knowledge addressed. As students progress in age, they are expected to know more information relative to a standard. Another difference between one level and the next is the introduction of new topics. For example, the benchmarks in Level I articulate information about the products of heat and describe features of the sun as a heat source for the earth. Level II provides information about the transfer of heat, the importance of mechanical and electrical energy as sources of heat, and the reciprocal relationship between heat and light. One might argue that all this information is roughly related to the topic of heat. Yet, it is also true that they represent topics in their own right. Level III seems to diverge even further, shifting the major emphasis from heat to energy. This change in emphasis is carried over to Level IV.

From this example one might conclude that, within the modern standards movement, the criteria for spiraling benchmarks from one level to the next seem to be the addition of information about a given topic and the addition of related topics. Although such an approach is not necessarily bad, the New Taxonomy allows those designing standards and benchmarks to more specifi-

Level I (Grades K-2)

- Knows that the sun applies heat and light to earth
- Knows that heat can be produced in many ways (e.g., burning, rubbing, mixing chemicals)

Level II (Grades 3-5)

- Knows that things that give off light often also give off heat
- Knows that mechanical and electrical machines give off heat
- Knows that heat can move from one object to another by conduction

Level III (Grades 6-8)

- Knows that energy comes in different forms, such as light, heat, chemical, nuclear, mechanical, and electrical
- Understands that energy cannot be created or destroyed, but only changed from one to another
- Knows that the Sun is a major source of energy for changes on the earth's surface; the sun's energy arrives as light with a range of wavelengths consisting mainly of visible light with significant amounts of infrared and ultraviolet radiation
- Knows that heat energy moves in predictable ways, flowing from warmer objects to cooler ones until both objects are at the same temperature

Level IV (Grades 9-12)

- Knows that although energy can be transferred by collisions or waves and converted from one form to another, it can never be created or destroyed, so the total energy of the universe is constant
- Knows that all energy can be considered to be either kinetic energy (energy of motion), potential energy (depends on relative position), or energy contained by a field (electromagnetic waves)
- Knows that heat energy consists of random motion and the vibrations of atoms, molecules, and ions; the higher the temperature, the greater the atomic or molecular motion
- Knows that energy tends to move spontaneously from hotter to cooler objects by conduction, convection, or radiation; similarly, any ordered state tends to spontaneously become less ordered over time
- Knows that electricity in circuits can produce light, heat, sound, and magnetic effects

Figure 6.2. Interval Benchmarks for Science Standard *(continued)*

- Knows that some materials conduct heat better than others; materials that do not conduct heat well can reduce heat loss
- Knows that electrical circuits require a complete loop through which the electrical current can pass
- Knows that heat can be transferred through materials by the collisions of atoms or across space by radiation; if the material is fluid, currents will be set up in it that aid the transfer of heat
- Knows that electrical circuits provide a means of converting electrical energy into heat, light, sound, chemical, or other forms of energy
- Knows that in most chemical reactions, energy is released or added to the system in the form of heat, light, electrical, or mechanical energy
- Knows that energy of waves (electromagnetic and material) can be changed into other forms of energy (e.g., chemical and electrical), just as other forms of energy (chemical and nuclear) can be transformed into wave energy
- Knows that some changes of atomic or molecular configuration require an input of energy, whereas others release energy
- Knows that each kind of atom or molecule can gain or lose energy in particular discrete amounts and thus can absorb and emit light only at wavelengths corresponding to these amounts; these wavelengths can be used to identify the substance
- Knows that fission is the splitting of a large nucleus into smaller pieces, and fusion is the joining of two nuclei at extremely high temperature and pressure; nuclear reactions convert a fraction of the mass of interacting particles into energy

Figure 6.2. Continued

cally identify the levels of understanding expected of students within a single topic. This might be a great aid in distinguishing expectations about benchmarks from one grade level to the next. To illustrate, consider the information about heat articulated in the Level II benchmarks in Figure 6.2. The expectation is that this content should be understood by students "by the end of grade 5." Figure 6.2, however, provides no guidance as to what should be addressed at third grade as opposed to fourth as opposed to fifth. Using the New Taxonomy, the expectation might be that by the end of third grade, students master the content about heat at the level of comprehension—they can articulate and represent the relationship among the defining elements of that information. By the end of fourth grade, students might be expected to have mastered the information at the level of analysis—they can make valid inferences based on it and identify errors in its application. Finally, by the end of fifth grade, they might be expected to have mastered the content at the level of utilization—they can use it to solve problems, make decisions, and so on.

The New Taxonomy, then, can help define the spiral nature of standards in the various subject areas. Stated differently, the New Taxonomy allows for the design of a spiral curriculum in a manner that goes beyond the simple addition of detail or addition of topics.

As a Tool for Planning Assessments

A final use of the New Taxonomy is as a tool for planning assessments. Recent years have seen an expansion of the various types of data considered as valid assessments. To illustrate, each of the following types of data are currently being used as assessments in K-12 classrooms:

1. forced-choice items

2. essays and oral reports

3. pictographs, graphic organizers, charts, and graphs

4. performance tasks

5. teacher observations

It should be noted that the term *assessment* is being used in a specific way here. Indeed, before discussing the use of the New Taxonomy as a tool for assessment design, it is useful to define some common terms:

Assessment: Gathering information about students' achievement or behavior

Evaluation: The process of making judgments about the level of students' understanding or performance

Measurement: Assigning marks based on an explicit set of rules

Score(s): The number or letter assigned to an assessment via the process of measurement. The term "mark" is commonly used synonymously with the term "score."

Grades: The number or letter reported at the end of a set period of time as a summary statement of evaluations made of students.

As defined here, assessment is the collection of data that are used to make judgments (i.e., evaluations) about students where judgment involves some kind of placement on a scale (i.e., measurement). With this in mind, it can be said that different types of assessment are most appropriate for different types of knowledge at different levels of the New Taxonomy.

In this section we address this issue for each of the five types of assessment listed above. It is also important to note that our discussion will address only the most appropriate use of these assessments. That is, it is probably true that any type of assessment could be made to work with any type of knowledge at any level of the New Taxonomy. However, the discussion below addresses the optimum use of an assessment type for a given domain of knowledge and level of the taxonomy.

Forced-Choice Items

Measurement expert Rick Stiggins (1994) defines forced-choice items in the following way:

> This is the classic objectively scored paper and pencil test. The respondent is asked a series of questions, each of which is accompanied by a range of alternative responses. The respondent's task is to select either the correct or best answer from among the options. The index of achievement is the number or proportion of questions answered correctly. (p. 84)

Stiggins lists four types of forced-choice items: (1) multiple-choice items, (2) true/false items, (3) matching exercises, and (4) short answer fill-in-the-blank items. As explained by Stiggins (1994), short-answer fill-in-the-blank items are counted in this category because they allow for only a single answer, which is counted either right or wrong. Teachers commonly use forced-choice items (along with essay items) to design their quizzes, homework assignments, midterm examinations, and final examinations. Such items play a major role in classroom assessment.

The utility of forced-choice items for the three knowledge domains across the six levels of the New Taxonomy is presented in Figure 6.3.

As depicted in Figure 6.3, forced-choice items are most appropriate for recall of information for all three types of knowledge. To illustrate, consider the following sample items:

Information:

A sodium ion differs from a sodium atom in that:

    a. It is an isotope of sodium.

    b. It is more reactive than a sodium atom.

	Information	Mental Procedures	Psychomotor Procedures
Level 6: Self			
Importance			
Efficacy			
Emotion			
Motivation			
Level 5: Metacognition			
Clarity			
Accuracy			
Goal Setting			
Process Monitoring			
Level 4: Knowledge Utilization			
Decision Making			
Problem Solving			
Experimental Inquiry			
Investigation			
Level 3: Analysis			
Matching			
Classification			
Error Analysis			
Induction			
Deduction			
Level 2: Comprehension			
Synthesis			
Representation			
Level 1: Retrieval			
Recall	✓	✓	✓
Execution			

Figure 6.3.   Forced-Choice Items

   c. It has a positive charge on its nucleus.

   d. It exists only in solution.

   e. It has fewer electrons.

Mental Procedures

Which of the following is the best description of the correct way to save a new file in WordPerfect?

   a. Use the mouse to click on the "File" command, then click on the "Save" command.

   b. The program automatically saves files when you exit.

   c. Type in the word *save* at the end of the file.

   d. After using the mouse to click on the "File" command, click on the "Save As" command.

Psychomotor Procedures

Which of the following is the best description of the correct way to hold a baseball to throw a curve ball?

   a. Keep index finger and middle finger wide apart and place them on smooth part of the ball.

   b. Keep index finger and middle finger close together and place them over the seams of the ball.

   c. Keep index finger and middle finger close together and place them over smooth part of the ball.

   d. Keep index finger and middle finger wide apart and place them over the seams of the ball.

Pictographs, Graphic Organizers, Charts, and Graphs

Pictographs, graphic organizers, charts, and graphs all emphasize nonlinguistic and symbolic representations of knowledge. The utility of these types of assessments for the three knowledge domains across the six levels of the New Taxonomy is depicted in Figure 6.4.

Given that pictographs, graphic representations, and the like all emphasize symbolic and nonlinguistic over linguistic depictions of knowledge, they are, by definition, appropriate vehicles for determining the extent to which students can accurately represent knowledge. For example, Figure 6.5 contains an illustration of how students might use a pictograph to represent their comprehension of the details about dictators.

	Information	*Mental Procedures*	*Psychomotor Procedures*
Level 6: Self			
Importance			
Efficacy			
Emotion			
Motivation			
Level 5: Metacognition			
Clarity			
Accuracy			
Goal Setting			
Process Monitoring			
Level 4: Knowledge Utilization			
Decision Making			
Problem Solving			
Experimental Inquiry			
Investigation			
Level 3: Analysis			
Matching	✓	✓	✓
Classification	✓	✓	✓
Error Analysis			
Induction			
Deduction			
Level 2: Comprehension			
Synthesis			
Representation	✓	✓	✓
Level 1: Retrieval			
Recall			
Execution			

Figure 6.4. Pictographs, Graphic Organizers, Charts, and Graphs

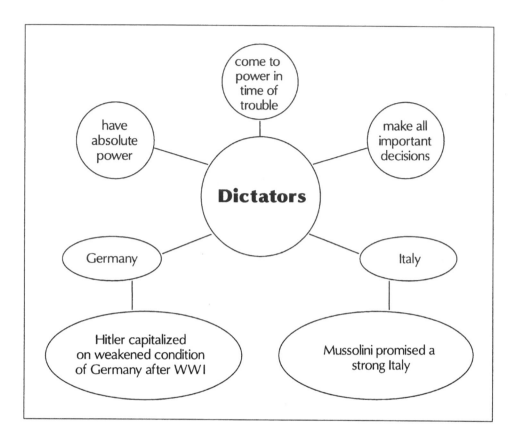

Figure 6.5. Representation for Dictators

As noted in Figure 6.4, some forms of graphic representations are highly useful for assessing student competency in the analysis processes of matching and classification, because both processes have specific types of graphic organizers devoted to them. To illustrate, Figure 6.6 contains an example of graphic organizers for matching and classification.

Essays and Oral Reports

Essays were probably the first form of assessment used in public education. Essays require students to construct their responses and are, therefore, highly useful for eliciting explanations. To help ensure that essays assess more than recall of information, the Center for Research on Evaluation, Standards, and Student Testing (CRESST) recommends that students be provided information that they can use and react to. To illustrate, CRESST provides students with the information in Figure 6.7 as part of a history essay question.

With this information as a backdrop to which all students have access, the following essay item is presented:

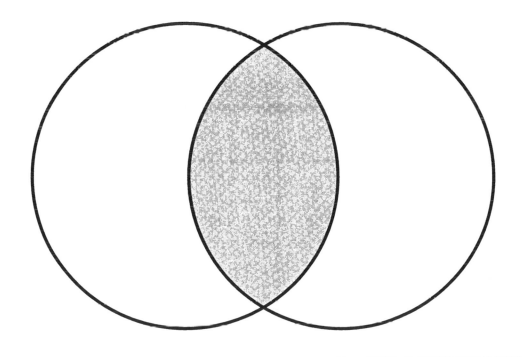

	Items to be compared			
Characteristics	#1	#2	#3	
1.				Similarities
				Differences
2.				Similarities
				Differences
3.				Similarities
				Differences
4.				Similarities
				Differences

Figure 6.6a. Matching

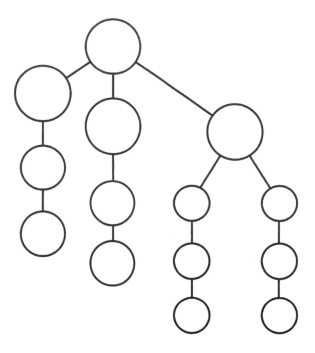

Categories

Figure 6.6b. Classifying

Excerpts from the Lincoln/Douglas Debate

Stephen A. Douglas

Mr. Lincoln tells you, in his speech made at Springfield, before the Convention which gave him his unanimous nomination, that

"A house divided against itself cannot stand."

"I believe this government cannot endure permanently, half slave and half free."

"I do not expect the Union to be dissolved, I don't expect the house to fall; but I do expect it will cease to be divided."

"It will become all one thing or all the other."

That is the fundamental principle upon which he sets out in this campaign. Well, I do not suppose you will believe one word of it when you come to examine it carefully, and see its consequences. Although the Republic has existed from 1789 to this day, divided into Free States and Slave States, yet we are told that in the future it cannot endure unless they shall become all free or all slave. For that reason he says . . .

Abraham Lincoln

Judge Douglas made two points upon my recent speech at Springfield. He says they are to be the issues of this campaign. The first one of these points he bases upon the language in a speech which I delivered at Springfield which I believe I can quote correctly from memory. I said there that "we are now far into the fifth year since a policy was instituted for the avowed object, and with the confident promise, of putting an end to slavery agitation; under the operation of that policy, that agitation had not only not ceased, but had constantly augmented." "I believe it will not cease until a crisis shall have been reached and passed. 'A house divided against itself cannot stand.' I believe this Government cannot endure permanently, half slave and half free." "I do not expect the Union to be dissolved"—I am quoting from my speech—"I do not expect the house to fall, but I do expect it will cease to be divided. It will become all one thing or the other. Either the opponents of slavery will arrest the spread of it and place it where the public mind shall rest, in the belief that it is in the course of ultimate extinction, or its advocates will push it forward until it shall become alike lawful in all the States, North as well as South. . . ."

Figure 6.7. Background for Essay Items

Imagine that it is 1858 and you are an educated citizen living in Illinois. Because you are interested in politics and always keep yourself well-informed, you make a special trip to hear Abraham Lincoln and Stephen Douglas debating during their campaigns for the Senate seat representing Illinois. After the debates you return home, where your cousin asks you about some of the problems that are facing the nation at this time.

Write an essay in which you explain the most important ideas and issues your cousin should understand (Baker, Aschbacher, Niemi, & Sato, 1992, p. 23).

Oral reports can be thought of as essays presented in oral form as opposed to written form. The same characteristics that make for a good essay task make for a good task designed to elicit an oral report.

The extent to which essays and oral reports can be used to assess different types of knowledge across the six levels of the New Taxonomy is presented in Figure 6.8.

As depicted in Figure 6.8, essays can effectively provide assessment data for almost all types of knowledge across almost every level of the New Taxonomy, because essays and oral reports are ideal vehicles for the explanations and presentations of evidence that are required for every element marked in Figure 6.8. For example, explanations are required of students if they are to demonstrate competence in the self-system process of examining importance. Recall from the discussion in Chapter 5 that a question that would elicit this type of thinking relative to the psychomotor process of playing defense in basketball is:

How important do you believe it is to be able to play defense in basketball? Why do you believe this and how valid is your thinking?

To respond to this question, students would have to not only provide an explanation, but would have to present a coherent argument for their explanation. Both aspects of the response could be communicated well via a written or oral report.

About the only aspects of the New Taxonomy for which essays and oral reports are not useful are the retrieval processes of recall and execution, and the comprehension process of representation. By definition, these processes do not require explanations.

Performance Tasks

Performance tasks have become very popular as tools for assessment. One of their defining characteristics is that they require students to construct their

	Information	Mental Procedures	Psychomotor Procedures
Level 6: Self			
Importance	✓	✓	✓
Efficacy	✓	✓	✓
Emotion	✓	✓	✓
Motivation	✓	✓	✓
Level 5: Metacognition			
Clarity	✓	✓	✓
Accuracy	✓	✓	✓
Goal Setting	✓	✓	✓
Process Monitoring	✓	✓	✓
Level 4: Knowledge Utilization			
Decision Making	✓	✓	✓
Problem Solving	✓	✓	✓
Experimental Inquiry	✓	✓	✓
Investigation	✓	✓	✓
Level 3: Analysis			
Matching	✓	✓	✓
Classification	✓	✓	✓
Error Analysis	✓	✓	✓
Induction	✓	✓	✓
Deduction	✓	✓	✓
Level 2: Comprehension			
Synthesis	✓	✓	✓
Representation			
Level 1: Retrieval			
Recall			
Execution			

Figure 6.8. Essays and Oral Reports

Geometry Task

Design packaging that will hold 576 cans of Campbell's Tomato Soup (net weight, 10 3/4 oz.) or packaging that will hold 144 boxes of Kellogg's Rice Krispies (net weight, 19 oz.). Use and list each individual package's real measurements; create scale drawings of front, top, and side perspectives; show the unfolded boxes/containers in a scale drawing; build a proportional, three-dimensional model.

Social Studies Task

Write a letter to a student living in South Central Los Angeles conveying your feeling about what happened in that area following the acquittal of police officers in the Rodney King case. Discuss the tension between our natural impulse to strike back at social injustice and the principles of nonviolence.

Figure 6.9. Performance Tasks

SOURCE: *A Guide to Authentic Instruction and Assessment: Vision, Standards and Scoring* (pp. 24-25), by F. M. Newmann, W. G. Secado, & G. G. Wehlage, 1995, Madison, WI: Wisconsin Center for Educational Research, University of Wisconsin.

responses and apply their knowledge (Meyer, 1992). To illustrate, consider the following performance tasks used by the National Assessment of Education Progress (for more examples, see Educational Testing Service, 1987).

1. Students are asked to describe what occurs when a drop of water is placed on each of seven different types of building materials. Next, they are asked to predict what will happen to a drop of water as it is placed on the surface of unknown material sealed in a plastic bag so that students can examine it but not test it.

2. Students are given a sample of three different materials and an open box. The samples differ in size, shape, and weight. The students are asked to determine whether the box would weigh the least (and the most) if it were filled completely with materials A, B, or C.

Researchers Fred Newmann, Walter Secado, and Gary Wehlage (1995) offer the examples in Figure 6.9 of performance tasks in geometry and social studies.

The extent to which performance tasks can be used to assess the three knowledge domains across the six levels of the New Taxonomy is depicted in Figure 6.10.

As depicted in Figure 6.10, performance tasks are useful for all types of knowledge across all levels of the New Taxonomy except for recall. One reason

	Information	Mental Procedures	Psychomotor Procedures
Level 6: Self			
Importance	✓	✓	✓
Efficacy	✓	✓	✓
Emotion	✓	✓	✓
Motivation	✓	✓	✓
Level 5: Metacognition			
Clarity	✓	✓	✓
Accuracy	✓	✓	✓
Goal Setting	✓	✓	✓
Process Monitoring	✓	✓	✓
Level 4: Knowledge Utilization			
Decision Making	✓	✓	✓
Problem Solving	✓	✓	✓
Experimental Inquiry	✓	✓	✓
Investigation	✓	✓	✓
Level 3: Analysis			
Matching	✓	✓	✓
Classification	✓	✓	✓
Error Analysis	✓	✓	✓
Induction	✓	✓	✓
Deduction	✓	✓	✓
Level 2: Comprehension			
Synthesis	✓	✓	✓
Representation	✓	✓	✓
Level 1: Retrieval			
Recall			
Execution		✓	✓

Figure 6.10. Performance Tasks

for this is that performance tasks commonly incorporate essays and oral reports. Therefore, performance tasks can address any type of knowledge and any aspect of the Taxonomy that can be assessed using essays and oral reports. In addition, performance tasks can be used to demonstrate the execution of skills and processes where essays and oral reports cannot. For example, in a performance task, students might be able to demonstrate their ability to perform a specific psychomotor process, whereas this would be difficult in an essay or oral report.

Teacher Observation

One of the most straightforward ways to collect assessment data is through informal observation of students. Researcher Audrey Kleinsasser (1991) explains that teacher observation involves the "informal conversations with students and observations of students that teachers make all day, every day" (p. 9). Reading expert Yetta Goodman refers to this as "kid watching" (Goodman, 1978; Wilde, 1996). Researcher Robert Calfee attests to the validity of teacher observation if teachers are highly knowledgeable about the subject area they are observing (Calfee, 1994; Calfee & Hiebert, 1991).

Quite simply, teacher observation involves making note of students' understanding of and competence in specific knowledge components as students go about their daily business. This is probably the most unobtrusive way of collecting assessment data because teachers do not design and administer specific assignments or tests. Stiggins (1994) provides the following example of how a teacher might observe a student relative to social interaction skills:

> A primary-grade teacher might watch a student interacting with classmates and draw inferences about that child's level of development in social interaction skills. If the levels of achievement are clearly defined in terms the observer can easily interpret, then the teacher, observing carefully, can derive information from watching that will aid in planning strategies to promote further social development. Thus, this is not an assessment where answers are counted right or wrong. Rather, like the essay test, we rely on teacher judgment to place the student's performance somewhere on a continuum of achievement levels ranging from very low to very high. (p. 160)

Figure 6.11 depicts the levels of the taxonomy for which teacher observation is most appropriate across the three knowledge domains.

Teacher observation is most appropriate for taxonomy processes that are easily observable over a short period of time. As Figure 6.11 illustrates, this

	Information	Mental Procedures	Psychomotor Procedures
Level 6: Self			
Importance			
Efficacy			
Emotion			
Motivation			
Level 5: Metacognition			
Clarity			
Accuracy			
Goal Setting			
Process Monitoring			
Level 4. Knowledge Utilization			
Decision Making			
Problem Solving			
Experimental Inquiry			
Investigation			
Level 3: Analysis			
Matching			
Classification			
Error Analysis			
Induction			
Deduction			
Level 2: Comprehension			
Synthesis	✓	✓	✓
Representation	✓	✓	✓
Level 1: Retrieval			
Recall	✓	✓	✓
Execution		✓	✓

Figure 6.11. Teacher Observation

limits its utility to retrieval and comprehension processes since evidence of these can be quickly observed. For example, while walking about the classroom, a teacher might informally observe that a student accurately reads a bar graph or remembers a specific detail. However, it would not be easy to incidentally observe the conclusions drawn by a student as a result of classifying information or engaging in experimental inquiry.

Epilogue

This volume has presented a New Taxonomy of educational objectives. However, as the title implies, it should be considered a first step in the design of a New Taxonomy. Though it has used the best available information regarding the nature of knowledge and the manner in which the human mind processes information, the New Taxonomy as described here will surely be revised over time. Educators are encouraged to use the New Taxonomy in ways they see fit, whether or not these ways are explicitly addressed in this book. Educators should also feel free to adapt the New Taxonomy—add to or delete from it—so as to make it most useful in their district, school, or classroom.

References

Airasian, P. W. (1987). State mandated testing and educational reform: Context and consequences. *American Journal of Education, 95*(3), 392-412.

Airasian, P. W. (1994). The impact of the taxonomy on testing and evaluation. In L. W. Anderson & L. A. Sosniak (Eds.), *Bloom's taxonomy: A forty-year retrospective: Ninety-third yearbook of the National Society for the Study of Education* (pp. 82-102). Chicago: University of Chicago Press.

Ajzen, I. (1985). From intentions to actions: A theory of planned behavior. In J. Kuhl & J. Beckman (Eds.), *Action-control: From cognition to behavior.* Heidelberg, Germany: Springer.

Ajzen, I., & Fishbein, M. (1977). Attitude-behavior relations: A theoretical analysis and review of empirical research. *Psychological Bulletin, 84,* 888-918.

Ajzen, I., & Fishbein, M. (1980). *Understanding attitudes and predicting social behavior.* Englewood Cliffs, NJ: Prentice Hall.

Ajzen, I., & Madden, T. J. (1986). Prediction of goal-directed behavior: Attitudes, intentions, and perceived behavioral control. *Journal of Experimental Social Psychology, 22,* 453-474.

Amabile, T. M. (1983). *The social psychology of creativity.* New York: Springer-Verlag.

Anderson, J. R. (1983). *The architecture of cognition.* Cambridge, MA: Harvard University Press.

Anderson, J. R. (1990a). *The adaptive character of thought.* Hillsdale, NJ: Lawrence Erlbaum.

Anderson, J. R. (1990b). *Cognitive psychology and its implications* (3rd ed.). New York: Freeman.

Anderson, J. R. (1995). *Learning and memory: An integrated approach.* New York: John Wiley.

Anderson, L. W., & Sosniak, L. A. (Eds.). (1994). *Bloom's taxonomy: A forty-year retrospective: Ninety-third yearbook of the National Society for the Study of Education.* Chicago: University of Chicago Press.

Baker, E. L., Aschbacher, P. R., Niemi, D., & Sato, E. (1992). *CRESST performance assessment models: Assessing content area explanations.* Los Angeles: University of California, Los Angeles: National Center for Research on Evaluation, Standards, and Student Testing.

Bandura, A. (1977). Self-efficacy: Toward a unifying theory of behavioral change. *Psychological Review, 84*(2), 191-215.

Bandura, A. (1982). Self-efficacy mechanism in human agency. *American Psychologist, 37,* 122-147.

Bandura, A. (1991). Social cognitive theory of self-regulation. *Organizational Behavior and Human Decision Processes, 50,* 248-287.

Bandura, A. (1993). Perceived self-efficacy in cognitive development and functioning. *Educational Psychologist, 28,* 117-148.

Bandura, A. (1996). Ontological and epistemological terrains revisited. *Journal of Behavior Therapy and Experimental Psychiatry, 27,* 323-345.

Bandura, A. (1997). *Self-efficacy: The exercise of control.* New York: Freeman.

Baron, J. (1982). Personality and intelligence. In R. J. Sternberg (Ed.), *Handbook of human intelligence* (pp. 308-351). London: Cambridge University Press.

Baron, J. (1985). Assessing higher order thinking skills in Connecticut. In C. P. Kearney (Ed.), *Assessing higher order thinking skills* (ERIC/TIME Resort 90). Princeton, NJ: Educational Testing Service.

Beyer, B. K. (1988). *Developing a thinking skills program.* Boston: Allyn & Bacon.

Bloom, B. S. (1976). *Human characteristics and school learning.* New York: McGraw-Hill.

Bloom, B. S., Engelhart, M. D., Furst, E. J., Hill, W. H., & Krathwohl, D. R. (Eds.). (1956). *Taxonomy of educational objectivities: The classification of educational goals. Handbook I: Cognitive domain.* New York: David McKay.

Braine, M. D. S. (1978). On the relation between the natural logic of reasoning and standard logic. *Psychological Review, 85,* 1-21.

Brown, A. L. (1978). Knowing when, where and how to remember: A problem of metacognition. In R. Glaser (Ed.), *Advances in instructional psychology* (Vol. 1, pp. 77-165). Hillsdale, NJ: Lawrence Erlbaum.

Brown, A. L. (1980). Metacognitive development and reading. In R. J. Spiro, B. C. Bruce, & W. F. Brewer (Eds.), *Theoretical issues in reading comprehension.* Hillsdale, NJ: Lawrence Erlbaum.

Brown, A. L. (1984). Metacognition, executive control, self-regulation, and other even more mysterious mechanisms. In F. E. Weinert & R. H. Kluwe (Eds.), *Metacognition, motivation, and learning* (pp. 60-108). Stuttgart, West Germany: Kuhlhammer.

Bruner, J. 1960. *The process of education.* Cambridge, MA: Harvard University Press.

Buber, M. (1958). *I and thou.* New York: Scribner.

Calfee, R. C. (1994). *Implications for cognitive psychology for authentic assessment and instruction* (Tech. Rep. No. 69). Berkeley, CA: University of California, National Center for the Study of Writing.

Calfee, R. C., & Hiebert, E. H. (1991). Classroom assessment of reading. In R. Barr, M. Kamil, P. Mosenthal, & P. D. Pearson (Eds.), *Handbook of research on reading* (2nd ed., pp. 281-309). New York: Longman.

Carroll, J. B. (1993). *Human cognitive abilities: A survey of factor-analytic studies*. New York: Cambridge University Press.

Chafe, W. L. (1970). *Meaning and structure of language*. Chicago: University of Chicago Press.

Clark, H. H., & Clark, E. V. (1977). *Psychology and language*. San Diego, CA: Harcourt Brace Jovanovich.

Clarke, J. H. (1991). Using visual organizers to focus on thinking. *Journal of Reading, 34*(7), 526-534.

College Board (1983). *Academic preparation for college: What students need to know and be able to do*. New York: College Entrance Examination Board.

Cooper, C. R. (1983). Procedures for describing written texts. In P. Mosenthal, L. Tamor, & S. A. Walmsley (Eds.), *Research on writing* (pp. 287-313). New York: Longman.

Costa, A. (1984). Mediating the metacognitive. *Educational Leadership, 42*(3), 57-62.

Costa, A. L. (1991). Toward a model of human intellectual functioning. In A. L. Costa (Ed.), *Developing minds: A resource book for teaching thinking* (rev. ed.). Alexandria, VA: Association for Supervision and Curriculum Development.

Dale, E. (1967). Historical setting of programmed instruction. In P. C. Lange (Ed.), *Programmed instruction: Sixty-sixth yearbook of the National Society for the Study of Education, part 2*. Chicago: University of Chicago Press.

de Beaugrande, R. (1980). *Text, discourse and process: Toward a multidisciplinary science of text*. Norwood, NJ: Ablex.

Deely, J. (1982). *Semiotics: Its history and doctrine*. Bloomington, IN: Indiana University Press.

Dennett, D. C. (1969). *Content and consciousness*. London: Routledge & Kegan Paul.

Dennett, D. C. (1991). *Consciousness explained*. Boston: Little, Brown.

Eco, U. (1976). *A theory of semiotics*. Bloomington, IN: Indiana University Press.

Eco, U. (1979). *The role of the reader*. Bloomington, IN: Indiana University Press.

Eco, U. (1984). *Semiotics and the philosophy of language*. Bloomington, IN: Indiana University Press.

Education Commission of the States. (1982). *The information society: Are high school graduates ready?* Denver, CO: Education Commission of the States.

Education Testing Service (1987). *Learning by doing: A manual for teaching and assessing higher order thinking in science and mathematics*. Princeton, NJ: Educational Testing Service.

Ehrenberg, S. D., Ehrenberg, L. M., & Durfee, D. (1979). *BASICS: Teaching/learning strategies*. Miami Beach, FL: Institute for Curriculum and Instruction.

Ennis, R. H. (1985). Goals for a critical thinking curriculum. In A. L. Costa (Ed.), *Developing minds: A resource book for teaching thinking* (pp. 54-57). Alexandria, VA: Association for Supervision and Curriculum Development.

Ennis, R. H. (1987a, Summer). A conception of critical thinking with some curriculum suggestions. *American Philosophical Association Newsletter on the Teaching of Philosophy*, pp. 1-5.

Ennis, R. H. (1987b). A taxonomy of critical thinking dispositions and abilities. In J. Baron & R. Sternberg (Eds.), *Teaching thinking skills: Theory and practice*. New York: Freeman.

Ennis, R. H. (1989). Critical thinking and subject specificity: Clarification and needed research. *Educational Researcher, 18*(3), 4-10.

Fairbrother, R. W. (1975). The reliability of teachers' judgments of the ability being tested by multiple-choice items. *Educational Researcher, 17*(3), 202-210.

Fillmore, C. J. (1968). The case for case. In E. Beck & R. T. Harms (Eds.), *Universals in linguistic theory* (pp. 1-210). New York: Holt, Rinehart & Winston.

Fitts, P. M. (1964). Perceptual-motor skill learning. In A. W. Melton (Ed.), *Categories of human learning*. New York: John Wiley.

Flavell, J. H. (1976). Metacognitive aspects of problem solving. In L. B. Resnick (Ed.), *The nature of intelligence*. Hillsdale, NJ: Lawrence Erlbaum.

Flavell, J. H. (1977). *Cognitive development*. Englewood Cliffs, NJ: Prentice Hall.

Flavell, J. H. (1978). Metacognitive development. In J. M. Scandura & C. J. Brainerd (Eds.), *Structural-process theories of complex human behavior* (pp. 213-245). Alpen a.d. Rijn, The Netherlands: Sijithoff and Noordhoff.

Flavell, J. H. (1979). Metacognition and cognitive monitoring: A new area of psychological inquiry. *American Psychologist, 34*, 906-911.

Flavell, J. H. (1987). Speculations about the nature and development of metacognition. In F. E. Weinert & R. H. Kluwe (Eds.), *Metacognition, motivation and understanding* (pp. 21-29). Hillside, NJ: Lawrence Erlbaum.

Frankl, V. E. (1967). *Psychotherapy and existentialism*. New York: Pocket Books.

Frederiksen, C. H. (1975). Representing logical and semantic structure of knowledge acquired from discourse. *Cognitive Psychology, 7*, 371-458.

Frederiksen, C. H. (1977). Semantic processing units in understanding text. In R. O. Freedle (Ed.), *Discourse production and comprehension* (Vol. 1, pp. 57-88). Norwood, NJ: Ablex.

Furst, E. J. (1994). Bloom's taxonomy: Philosophical and educational issues. In L. W. Anderson & L. A. Sosniak (Eds.), *Bloom's taxonomy: A forty-year retrospective: Ninety-third yearbook of the National Society for the Study of Education* (pp. 28-40). Chicago: University of Chicago Press.

Gagne, R. M. (1977). *The conditions of learning* (3rd ed.). New York: Holt, Rinehart & Winston.

Gagne, R. M. (1989). *Studies of learning: 50 years of research*. Tallahassee: Florida State University, Learning Systems Institute.

Garcia, T., & Pintrich, P. R. (1991, August). *The effects of autonomy on motivation, use of learning strategies, and performance in the college classroom.*

Paper presented at the annual meeting of the American Psychological Association, San Francisco, CA.

Garcia, T., & Pintrich, P. R. (1993, August). *Self-schemas as goals and their role in self-regulated learning.* Paper presented at the annual meeting of the American Psychological Association, Toronto, Canada.

Garcia, T., & Pintrich, P. R. (1995, August). *The role of possible selves in adolescents' perceived competence and self-regulation.* Paper presented at the annual meeting of the American Educational Research Association, San Francisco, CA.

Gentner, D., & Markman, A. B. (1994). Structural alignment in comparison: No difference without similarity. *Psychological Science, 5*(3), 152-158.

Gilovich, T. (1991). *How we know what isn't so.* New York: Free Press.

Goodman, Y. M. (1978). Kid watching: An alternative to testing. *National Elementary School Principal, 57,* 41-45.

Halpern, D. F. (1984). *Thought and knowledge: An introduction to critical thinking.* Hillsdale, NJ: Lawrence Erlbaum.

Harter, S. (1980). The perceived competence scale for children. *Child Development, 51,* 218-235.

Hayes, J. R. (1981). *The complete problem solver.* Philadelphia: The Franklin Institute.

Heimlich, J. E., & Pittelman, S. D. (1988). *Semantic mapping: Classroom applications.* Newark, DE: International Reading Association.

Hirsch, E. D., Jr. (1996). *The schools we need: Why we don't have them.* New York: Doubleday.

Holland, J. H., Holyoak, K. F., Nisbett, R. E., & Thagard, P. R. (1986). *Induction: Processes of inference, learning, and discovery.* Cambridge: MIT Press.

Johnson-Laird, P. N. (1983). *Mental models.* Cambridge, MA: Harvard University Press.

Johnson-Laird, P. N., & Byrne, R. M. J. (1991). *Deduction.* Hillsdale, NJ: Lawrence Erlbaum.

Jones, B. F., Amiran, M., & Katims, M. (1985). Teaching cognitive strategies and text structures within language arts programs. In J. W. Segal, S. F. Chipman, & R. Glaser (Eds.), *Thinking and learning skills, Vol. 1: Relating instruction to research* (pp. 259-295). Hillsdale, NJ: Lawrence Erlbaum.

Jones, B. F., Palincsar, A. S., Ogle, D. S., & Carr, E. G. (1987). *Strategic teaching: Cognitive instruction in the content areas.* Alexandria, VA: Association of Supervision and Curriculum Development.

Kintsch, W. (1974). *The representation of meaning in memory.* Hillsdale, NJ: Lawrence Erlbaum.

Kintsch, W. (1979). On modeling comprehension. *Educational psychologist, 1,* 3-14.

Kleinsasser, A. (1991, September). *Rethinking assessment: Who's the expert?* Paper presented at the Casper Outcomes Conference, Casper, WY.

Kreitzer, A. E., & Madaus, G. F. (1994). Empirical investigations of the hier-
    archial structure of the taxonomy. In L. W. Anderson & L. A. Sosniak (Eds.),
    *Bloom's taxonomy: A forty-year retrospective: Ninety-third yearbook of the
    National Society for the Study of Education* (pp. 64-81). Chicago: Univer-
    sity of Chicago Press.

LaBerge, D., & Samuels, S. J. (1974). Toward a theory of automatic information
    processing in reading. In H. Singer & R. B. Riddell (Eds.), *Theoretical mod-
    els and processes of reading* (pp. 548-579). Newark, DE: International
    Reading Association.

LaBerge, D. L. (1995). *Attentional processing: The brain's art of mindfulness.*
    Cambridge, MA: Harvard University Press.

LeDoux, J. E. (1996). *The emotional brain: The mysterious underpinnings of
    emotional life.* New York: Simon & Schuster.

Lindsay, P. H., & Norman, D. A. (1977). *Human information processing.* New
    York: Academic Press.

Madaus, G. F., & Stufflebeam, D. (Eds.). (1989). *Educational evaluation: Classic
    works of Ralph W. Tyler.* Boston: Kluwer Academic Press.

Mager, R. (1962). *Preparing instructional objectives.* Palo Alto, CA: Fearon.

Mandler, G. (1983). The nature of emotions. In J. Miller (Ed.), *States of mind*
    (pp. 136-153). New York: Pantheon.

Markman, A. B., & Gentner, D. (1993a). Splitting the differences: A structural
    alignment view of similarity. *Journal of Memory and Learning, 32,* 517-535.

Markman, A. B., & Gentner, D. (1993b). Structural alignment during similarity
    comparisons. *Cognitive Psychology, 25,* 431-467.

Markus, H., & Ruvulo, A. (1990). Possible selves: Personalized representations
    of goals. In L. Pervin (Ed.), *Goal concepts in psychology* (pp. 211-241).
    Hillsdale, NJ: Lawrence Erlbaum.

Marzano, R. J. (1992). *A different kind of classroom: Teaching with Dimensions
    of Learning.* Alexandria, VA: Association for Supervision and Curriculum
    Development.

Marzano, R. J. (1998). *A theory-based meta-analysis of research on instruction*
    (Technical Report). Aurora, CO: Mid-continent Regional Educational
    Laboratory.

Marzano, R. J., Brandt, R. S., Hughes, C. S., Jones, B. F., Presseisen, B. Z.,
    Rankin, S. C., & Suhor, C. (1988). *Dimensions of thinking: A framework for
    curriculum and instruction.* Alexandria, VA: Association for Supervision
    and Curriculum Development.

Marzano, R. J., & Kendall, J. S. (1996a). *A comprehensive guide to designing
    standards-based districts, schools, and classrooms.* Alexandria, VA: Associ-
    ation for Supervision and Curriculum Development.

Marzano, R. J., & Kendall, J. S. (1996b). *The fall and rise of standards-based
    education.* Alexandria, VA: National Association of State Boards of
    Education.

Marzano, R. J., Kendall, J. S., & Cicchinelli, L. F. (1998). *What Americans believe students should know: A survey of U. S. adults.* Aurora, CO: Mid-continent Regional Educational Laboratory.

Marzano, R. J., Kendall, J. S., & Gaddy, B. B. (1999). *Essential knowledge: The debate over what American students should know.* Aurora, CO: Mid-continent Regional Educational Laboratory.

Marzano, R. J., Pickering, D. J., Arredondo, D. E., Blackburn, G. J., Brandt, R. S., Moffett, C. A., Paynter, D. E., Pollock, J. E., & Whisler, J. S. (1997). *Dimensions of learning: Teacher's manual* (2nd ed.). Alexandria, VA: Association for Supervision and Curriculum Development.

Maslow, A. H. (1968). *Toward a psychology of being.* New York: Van Nostrand Reinhold.

McTighe, J., & Lyman, F. T., Jr. (1988). Cueing thinking in the classroom: The promise of theory embedded tools. *Educational Leadership, 45*(7), 18-25.

Medawar, P. B. (1967). Two conceptions of science. In J. P. Medawar (Ed.), *The art of the soluble.* London: Methuen.

Medin, D., Goldstone, R. L., & Markman, A. B. (1995). Comparison and choice: Relations between similarity processes and decision processes. *Psychonomic Bulletin & Review, 2*(1), 1-19.

Meichenbaum, D., & Asarnow, J. (1979). Cognitive-behavioral modification and metacognitive development: Implications for the classroom. In P. C. Kendall & S. D. Hollon (Eds.), *Cognitive-behavioral interventions: Theory, research, and procedures* (pp. 11-35). New York: Academic.

Mervis, C. B. (1980). Category structure and the development of categorization. In R. J. Spiro, B. C. Bruce, & W. F. Brewer (Eds.), *Theoretical issues in reading comprehension* (pp. 279-307). Hillsdale, NJ: Lawrence Erlbaum.

Meyer, B. J. F. (1975). *The organization of prose and its effects on memory.* New York: American Elsevier.

Meyer, C. A. (1992). What's the difference between authentic and performance assessment? *Educational Leadership, 49*(8), 39-40.

Murphy, P. D. (1974). *Consumer education modules: A spiral process approach.* North Dakota State University, Fargo, Curriculum Development in Vocational and Technical Education. Washington, DC: Office of Education.

National Commission on Excellence in Education. (1983). *A nation at risk: The imperative for educational reform.* Washington, DC: Government Printing Office.

National Education Goals Panel. (1991). *The national education goals report: Building a nation of learners.* Washington, DC: Author.

Newmann, F. M., Secado, W. G., & Wehlage, G. G. (1995). *A guide to authentic instruction and assessment: Vision, standards and scoring.* Madison: University of Wisconsin, Wisconsin Center for Educational Research.

Nickerson, R. S., Perkins, D. N., & Smith, E. E. (1985). *The teaching of thinking.* Hillsdale, NJ: Lawrence Erlbaum.

Norman, D. A., & Rumelhart, D. E. (1975). *Explanations in cognition.* New York: Freeman.

Paivio, A. (1969). Mental imagery in associative learning and memory. *Psychological Review, 76,* 241-263.

Paivio, A. (1971). *Imagery and verbal processing.* New York: Holt, Rinehart & Winston.

Paris, S. G., Lipson, M. Y., & Wixson, K. K. (1983). Becoming a strategic reader. *Contemporary Educational Psychology, 8*(3), 293-316.

Paul, R. (1990). *Critical thinking: What every person needs to survive in a rapidly changing world.* Rohnert Park, CA: Center for Critical Thinking and Moral Critique, Sonoma State University.

Paul, R. W. (1984). Critical thinking: Fundamental to education for a free society. *Educational Leadership, 42*(1), 4-14.

Paul, R. W. (1986a, December). *Critical thinking, moral integrity, and citizenship: Teaching for the intellectual virtues.* Paper distributed at ASCD Wingspread Conference on Teaching Skills, Racine, WI.

Paul, R. W. (1986b). *Program for the fourth international conference on critical thinking and educational reform.* Rohnert Park, CA: Sonoma State University, Center for Critical Thinking and Moral Critique.

Percy, W. (1975). *The message in the bottle.* New York: Farrar, Strauss & Giroux.

Perkins, D. N. (1984). Creativity by design. *Educational Leadership, 42*(1), 18-25.

Perkins, D. N. (1985). *Where is creativity?* Paper presented at University of Iowa Second Annual Humanities Symposium, Iowa City, IA.

Perkins, D. N. (1986). *Knowledge as design.* Hillsdale, NJ: Lawrence Erlbaum.

Piaget, J. (1971). *Genetic epistemology* (E. Duckworth, Trans.). New York: Norton.

Pintrich, P. R., & Garcia, T. C. (1992, April). *An integrated model of motivation and self-regulated learning.* Paper presented at the annual meeting of the American Educational Research Association, San Francisco, CA.

Poole, R. L. (1972). Characteristics of the taxonomy of educational objectives, cognitive domain: A replication. *Psychology in the Schools, 9*(1), 83-88.

Richardson, A. (1983). Imagery: Definitions and types. In A. A. Sheikh (Ed.), *Imagery: Current theory, research, and application* (pp. 3-42). New York: John Wiley.

Richardson, A. (1983). Images, definitions and types. In A. A. Sheikh (Ed.), *Imagery: Current theory, research, and application.* New York: John Wiley.

Rohwer, W. D., & Sloane, K. (1994). Psychological perspectives. In L. W. Anderson & L. A. Sosniak (Eds.), *Bloom's taxonomy: A forty-year retrospective: Ninety-third yearbook of the National Society for the Study of Education* (pp. 41-63). Chicago: University of Chicago Press.

Ross, J. A. (1988). Controlling variables: A meta-analysis of training studies. *Review of Educational Research, 58*(4), 405-437.

Rowe, H. (1985). *Problem solving and intelligence.* Hillsdale, NJ: Lawrence Erlbaum.

Rumelhart, D. E., & Norman, D. A. (1981). Accretion, tuning and restructuring: Three modes of learning. In J. W. Colton & R. Klatzky (Eds.), *Semantic factors in cognition.* Hillsdale, NJ: Lawrence Erlbaum.

Salomon, G., & Globerson, T. (1987). Skill may not be enough: The role of mindfulness in learning and transfer. *International Journal of Educational Research, 11,* 623-637.

Schank, R. C., & Abelson, R. (1977). *Scripts, plans, goals and understanding.* Hillsdale, NJ: Lawrence Erlbaum.

Seligman, M. E. P. (1990). *Learned optimism.* New York: Pocket Books.

Seligman, M. E. P. (1994). *What you can change and what you can't.* New York: Knopf.

Shepard, L. (1993). *Setting performance standards for student achievement: A report of the National Academy of Education Panel on the evaluation of the NAEP trial state assessment: An evaluation of the 1992 achievement levels.* Stanford, CA: Stanford University, The National Academy of Education.

Smith, E. E., & Medin, D. L. (1981). *Categories and concepts.* Cambridge, MA: Harvard University Press.

Snow, R. E., & Lohman, D. F. (1989). Implications of cognitive psychology for educational measurement. In R. L. Linn (Ed.), *Educational measurement* (3rd ed., pp. 263-331). New York: American Council on Education and Macmillan Publishing Company.

Snowman, J., & McCown, R. (1984, April). *Cognitive processes in learning: A model for investigating strategies and tactics.* Paper presented at the annual meeting of the American Educational Research Association, New Orleans, LA.

Stahl, R. J. (1985). *Cognitive information processes and processing within a uniprocess superstructure/microstructure framework: A practical information-based model.* Unpublished manuscript, University of Arizona, Tucson.

Stanley, J. C., & Bolton, D. (1957). A review of Bloom's taxonomy of educational objectives and J. R. Gerberich's specimen objective test items: A guide to achievement test construction. *Educational and Psychological Measurement, 17*(4), 631-634.

Sternberg, R. J. (1987). Most vocabulary is learned from context. In M. G. McKeown & M. E. Curtis (Eds.), *The nature of vocabulary acquisition* (pp. 89-105). Hillsdale, NJ: Lawrence Erlbaum.

Sternberg, R. J. (1977). *Intelligence, information processing and analogical reasoning: The componential analysis of human abilities.* Hillsdale, NJ: Lawrence Erlbaum.

Sternberg, R. J. (1984a). *Beyond IQ: A triarchic theory of human intelligence.* New York: Cambridge University Press.

Sternberg, R. J. (1984b). Mechanisms of cognitive development: A componential approach. In R. J. Sternberg (Ed.), *Mechanisms of cognitive development* (pp. 163-186). New York: Freeman.

Sternberg, R. J. (1986a). Inside intelligence. *American Scientist, 74,* 137-143.

Sternberg, R. J. (1986b). *Intelligence applied.* New York: Harcourt Brace Jovanovich.

Stiggins, R. J. (1994). *Student-centered classroom assessment.* New York: Merrill.

Taba, H. (1967). *Teacher's handbook for elementary social studies.* Reading, MA: Addison-Wesley.

Toulmin, S., Rieke, R., & Janik, A. (1981). *An introduction to reasoning.* New York: Macmillan.

Travers, R. M. W. (1950). *How to make achievement tests.* New York: Odyssey.

Turner, A., & Greene, E. (1977). *The construction of a propositional text base.* Boulder: The University of Colorado at Boulder, Institute for the Study of Intellectual Behavior.

van Dijk, T. A. (1977). *Text and context.* London: Longman.

van Dijk, T. A. (1980). *Macrostructures.* Hillsdale, NJ: Lawrence Erlbaum.

van Dijk, T. A., & Kintsch, W. (1983). *Strategies of discourse comprehension.* Hillsdale, NJ: Lawrence Erlbaum.

Wales, C. E., Nardi, A. H., & Stager, R. A. (1985). Teaching decision-making: What to teach and how to teach it. In A. L. Costa (Ed.), *Developing minds: A resource book for teaching thinking.* Alexandria, VA: Association for Supervision and Curriculum Development.

Wales, C. E., Nardi, A. H., & Stager, R. A. (1986). Decision making: New paradigm for education. *Educational Leadership, 43*(8), 37-41.

Wales, C. E., & Stager, R. A. (1977). *Guided design.* Morgantown: West Virginia University Center for Guided Design.

Wang, M. C., Haertel, G. D., & Walberg, H. J. (1993). Toward a knowledge base for school learning. *Review of Educational Research, 63*(3), 249-294.

Wilde, S. (Ed.). (1996). *Notes from a kid watcher: Selected writings of Yetta M. Goodman.* Portsmouth, NH: Heinemann.

Index

CORWIN
PRESS

The Corwin Press logo—a raven striding across an open book—represents the happy union of courage and learning. We are a professional-level publisher of books and journals for K–12 educators, and we are committed to creating and providing resources that embody these qualities. Corwin's motto is "Success for All Learners."